BARBECUE

BARBECUE

RECIPES • TECHNIQUES • TOOLS

CHRIS SCHLESINGER
& JOHN WILLOUGHBY

DK

LONDON NEW YORK MELBOURNE
MUNICH DELHI

Produced for Dorling Kindersley by

cobaltid

The Stables, Wood Farm, Deopham Road,
Attleborough, Norfolk NR17 1AJ
www.cobaltid.co.uk

ART EDITORS
Paul Reid, Lloyd Tilbury,
Darren Bland, Claire Dale

EDITORS
Louise Abbott,
Marek Walisiewicz, Kati Dye

PHOTOGRAPHY ART DIRECTION
Paul Reid

FOOD STYLIST
Gizzi Erskine

PHOTOGRAPHY
Ian O'Leary, with assistance
from Gemma Reynolds

For Dorling Kindersley

MANAGING EDITOR
Dawn Henderson

MANAGING ART EDITOR
Heather McCarry

EDITOR
Ariane Durkin

PROJECT ART EDITOR
Caroline de Souza

PRODUCTION EDITOR
Luca Frassinetti

PRODUCTION CONTROLLER
Mandy Inness

ANGLICIZATION EDITOR
Lee Faber

First published by Dorling Kindersley in 2008
The Penguin Group

2 4 6 8 10 9 7 5 3 1

Copyright © 2008 Dorling Kindersley Limited
Text copyright © 2008 Chris Schlesinger & John Willoughby
This paperback edition was published in 2011 by Dorling Kindersley

ISBN 978 1 4053 6650 2

Printed and bound in China by Hung Hing

Discover more at
www.dk.com

CONTENTS

FIRING UP

COOKING OVER LIVE FIRE IS FUN. BUT TO BE TRULY RELAXED AND CAREFREE AT THE GRILL, YOU NEED TO KNOW A FEW THINGS: HOW TO CHOOSE YOUR FUEL AND YOUR TOOLS, BUILD AND START THE FIRE, SEASON AND FLAVOUR YOUR FOOD, AND KNOW WHEN THE FOOD IS DONE. READ ON.

WHAT IS GRILLING?

We love grilling, because it's the most direct and straightforward of all cooking methods: you put some food over a fire and leave it there until it's cooked. So grilling appeals to us on an almost instinctive level – after all, we humans have been doing it pretty much since we climbed down from the trees. But the other thing that draws us to grilling (in addition, of course, to the wonderful flavour it gives to food) is that, despite its simplicity, it is also intriguingly complex. Each live fire you build is a little bit different from any other one that ever existed. This means that you have to pay attention – you have to react with that particular fire and the particular food you are cooking. So the process involves not only the atavistic joy of playing with fire, but also the appeal of a game that's just slightly different every time you play it. And it's even more than that.

To fully plumb the nature of this technique, it makes sense to look at it from three points of view, taking the best from each along the way. To most Americans, for example, grilling is not just a way of cooking food, it's a central part of a near-mythic social ritual known as the "backyard cookout". This culinary rite forms an important part of the American self-image, and as such is characterized by what are thought of as prototypically American attributes: casualness, informality, equality, and a kind of genial, low-key camaraderie. To underline the carefree, democratic nature of the occasion, the grilling at cookouts has traditionally been performed by dads, who at other times have tended to treat cooking as a foreign realm of endeavour. From this American model, grillers can take what is perhaps the single most important aspect of the method: it's just plain fun. But grilling has a long and distinguished history that far predates the USA. It is, in fact, a highly respected, bona fide cooking technique with a pedigree supplied by no less than Auguste Escoffier, the 19th-century French master chef who codified culinary techniques as practised in the West. In his seminal book, *Ma Cuisine*, Escoffier recognized grilling as "the remote starting point, the very genesis of our art".

But what should go over the flames? Although this has changed over the last couple of decades, the American idea of grilling food traditionally ran to burgers, steaks, and hot dogs — the type of food that even a novice dad had a fair chance of getting right. Escoffier was more adventurous, but leaned toward chops, steaks, and fish fillets draped in complex sauces. Fortunately, the cuisines of the hot-weather world contain a massive repertoire of imaginative grilled food. Even today, for a great many home cooks in these regions, cooking over live fire is neither a weekend ritual nor a professional technique — it's simply the way they cook every day. And they've been doing it for hundreds of years.

Here, then, grillers can find a whole new world of possibilities. Watching a fisherman grill freshly-caught sardines on a beach in southern Portugal, savouring skewers of grilled lamb in a side street in Istanbul or spicy prawns in a market in Saigon, munching on a crisp, flame-marked pappadum in Mumbai, or sitting down to a Middle Eastern *meze* with its grilled peppers, tomatoes, and aubergines, you realize that the possibilities for grilled food are virtually endless.

And there you have it. By extracting the best points from three distinct approaches, the modern griller becomes multidimensional — relaxed and casual, but technically expert and imaginative in menu choices. And, of course, you get to play with fire. So let's get grilling.

YOUR LIVE FIRE REPERTOIRE

People all over the world routinely cook with live fire, and they use all kinds of inventive methods when they do so. We think it's not only interesting but useful to know the differences between these various techniques. The best way to understand them, to us, is to look at what is being cooked, what temperature it is being cooked at, and why this method is the appropriate one for that food. In other words, it's good to understand the methods by looking at what you're trying to achieve.

GRILLING

Grilling basically involves cooking food quickly over the coals of a hot fire. When food is laid over the direct heat of the coals, a seared crust develops on the exterior. This flavour-packed crust (not the fuel) is most directly responsible for the characteristic taste of grilled food. On the other hand, the food also needs to be properly cooked on

The lid stays open for direct-heat cooking

A thick layer of coals will give you the intense heat you need

If cooking thick or bone-in cuts, tapering the coals toward the fire edge gives you an area of gentler heat to get interior doneness right without over-charring the outside

Coal-free area gives you somewhere to move food to in case of flare-ups

A FIRE FOR SIMPLE GRILLING
Depending on what you're planning to cook, you'll need to build either a simple or a multilevel fire (*see p30*). Start checking the temperature (*see p34*) as soon as the flames die down to catch the right moment to cook.

GRILLING: THE FACTS

- Fire temperature depends on what is being cooked
- Fast cooking, lid open
- What to grill: small, tender things; steaks, chops, baby back ribs; fish fillets, fish steaks, and other seafood; vegetables and fruits

SAMPLE RECIPES 1. New York Steak (*p60*); 2. Oriental Pork Ribs (*p88*); 3. Thai Chicken Satay (*p210*); 4. Halibut Steaks (*p120*); 5. Clams in Chilli-Butter Sauce (*p140*).

the inside by the time it comes off the grill. This relationship between surface sear and interior doneness, then, becomes the crux of the matter, the key to great grilled food. These are our top tips for perfect grilling:

- Build the right fire (*see pp30–1*) for the food you're going to grill.
- Before you put that food on the grill, be sure that you are cooking with the right temperature fire. Not everything should be cooked over the same heat, so always check the recipe and then see how hot the fire is (*see p34*) before you start cooking.
- Never cover the grill when you're doing direct-heat grilling (*see p35*).
- Start checking food for doneness (*see pp36–7*) well before you think it is actually ready to come off the grill. All live fires are different, so cooking times in recipes are just approximations, and checking for doneness early and often may just save you from a dry, overcooked dinner.

BARBECUING

This is where the terminology can be confusing. In much of the English-speaking world, including large parts of the United States, "barbecuing" and "grilling" are used interchangeably. But in the American South, "barbecue" describes a cooking method in which food is cooked slowly over the indirect heat and smoke from a charcoal or hardwood fire, which is quite different from cooking directly over the coals. The term is also used to describe the meat cooked by this method, which should always be both tender and smoky if you've done it right. Like braising, barbecuing was developed to deal with large, tough pieces of meat that need slow cooking over a low heat in order to become tender. The best-known US examples are the pork shoulder, favoured by North Carolina fans; beef brisket, the most popular barbecue of Texas; lamb shoulder, which you'll find most prominently in Kentucky; and ribs, which are found all through the southern half of the country.

The temperature of a barbecue pit should be somewhere between 80 and 115°C (180–240°F). As the meat basks in the low,

USING THE GRILL TO BARBECUE As the food is not directly above the coals, you don't, when the lid is closed, get a buildup of the acrid fumes caused when fat drips onto the fire (*see also p35*), so the meat won't be tainted by off flavours.

Heap the coals well up to one side of the grill. You don't need a lot of charcoal to produce gentle barbecuing heat

The food is always placed over the coal-free area

Closing the lid creates an oven-like cooking environment

Partially open the vents to keep the fire going yet retain the heat

BARBECUING: THE FACTS

- Low heat (80–115°C/ 180–240°F)
- Slow cooking, lid on
- What to cook: large, tough cuts of meat – racks of ribs, shoulder joints, beef brisket

SAMPLE RECIPES
1. Southern Slow-Cooked Pork (*p196*) 2. Texan Slow-Cooked Beef (*p180*) 3. Cuban Pork Ribs (*p46*).

smoky heat, the tough connective tissue in the meat – known as collagen – dissolves, and the meat itself goes from very tough to extremely tender. The technique of barbecuing involves building a fire on only one side of your grill, using about enough charcoal to fill a large shoebox, then putting the food on the other side and covering the grill. After that you just let it cook, adding a handful of coals every 30 minutes or so to keep the temperature in the proper range.

The technique of barbecuing is simple, requiring primarily patience, but it gives a remarkable end result, as generations of Southern barbecue cooks can testify. One more thing while we're talking barbecue: you don't use temperature to decide when your meat is ready to eat, because you are looking to go beyond mere doneness all the way to tenderness. Instead, use the "fork test": stick a large fork into whatever you're cooking and try to pick it up. If the fork slides out of the meat without grabbing onto it, it's done; otherwise, keep cooking.

TOPPING UP THE FIRE "Little and often" is the secret to keeping a good, slow barbecuing fire going. Some joints take 8 hours or more to cook, so be sure to lay in a good supply of charcoal to take you through the day (or night).

SMOKE-ROASTING

Next to grilling itself, this is the most useful of the live-fire cooking methods. It is similar to barbecuing, but you are cooking at a higher temperature, between 150 and 230°C (300–450°F). So when you build the fire on one side of your grill you use more charcoal than when barbecuing, enough to fill about 1½ shoeboxes, and when you add charcoal during refuelling, you use two handfuls rather than one. Basically what you are doing is roasting in a smoky environment. Like oven roasting, this method

Closing the lid keeps all that heat inside to roast the food

The joint or bird sits over the coal-free half of the grill, preventing fat flare-ups and acrid fumes

is most suitable for large, relatively tender foods – beef and pork joints, leg of lamb, chickens, turkeys, ducks, whole fish, and basically anything else you would put in the oven if you were cooking inside. But you have the additional advantage that whatever you're cooking will pick up that ineffable smoky flavour from the charcoal or wood you're burning.

SMOKE-ROASTING ON THE GRILL
A deep layer of coals over half the base of the grill (*see left and top of page*) gives you your initial high heat; to keep this going, you need to top the fire up generously every half-hour or so.

SMOKE-ROASTING: THE FACTS

- Hot fire (150–230°C / 300–450°F)
- Medium to long cooking times, lid on
- What to cook: large but tender, juicy joints; whole birds and fish

SAMPLE RECIPES 1. Glazed Roast Leg of Pork (*p204*) 2. Smoke-Roasted Whole Duck (*p200*); 3. Pepper-Crusted Smoke-Roasted Beef (*p194*).

ASH-ROASTING IN FOIL Lots of vegetables grill well, but ash-roasting gives your side dishes a melting, succulent texture to contrast with the seared crust of a grilled steak or chop.

ASH-ROASTING

Since ancient times, people have been encasing food in leaves and putting it in a pit with coals to cook. It is still fairly widely used today – think of the Hawaiian *luau* or the *pibil* of Mexico. Ash-roasting, also known as "hobo pack cooking" (the Boy Scout name for it), is really just a variation on this method. Instead of leaves, you wrap the food in foil; instead of a coal-lined pit, you simply slide it into the coals of your fire. It's pretty much as simple as that, but there are two important things to remember. First, be sure that there is a good amount of liquid in the parcel, otherwise the food will dry out in those hot coals. Second, wrap the foil carefully, so that juices don't leak out. The package doesn't need to be dug down into the coals so it's completely covered. Instead, just push it in so the coals come part-way up the sides. This technique is particularly useful because you can cook your side dishes – or even your dessert – in the coals while other food is cooking above them.

WHAT'S THE BEST GRILL FOR YOU?

We've grilled on a $5,000 super-behemoth gas grill, an oven rack perched on three rocks, and pretty much everything in between. And what we've learned is that the most important thing is technique, not equipment. In addition, we know that the particular grill that you choose is largely a matter of **personal preference**, **budget**, and **available space**. Having said all that, though, we have found, over many years, that there are a couple of grill qualities that can make grilling easier and more successful.

First, it is best to get **a covered grill**. While you can do a fine job grilling on a hibachi, you need that cover for any of the other live-fire cooking techniques, such as smoke-roasting or barbecuing. It's even more important to get a grill with **a generous grilling surface**. A couple of years ago I (Chris) got a giant charcoal grill, 120cm (48in) in diameter, and I've become addicted to it. It lets me entertain a crowd without having to cook in stages. It also makes it possible to have a wide range of heat: I can be searing steaks over **a hot fire on one side**, and slow-cooking tomatoes over **a low fire on the other**, while still having a space with no coals at all in case I need to move something there to **quickly cool down**. In other words, it just gives me the most **versatility**. Of course, you may not have room in your garden (or your budget) for a grill this giant, but we strongly recommend: when buying a grill, get the largest one you can accommodate. You need a grill grid at least **55cm (22in) across** for anything but the simplest, most direct grilling. One other feature that's worth looking for is **a grill rack with a hinged lid** so it's easy to add more charcoal during cooking – particularly useful for smoke-roasting.

WHAT TO LOOK FOR Space for tools (1) is always handy; titanic gas grills (2) often feature warming areas, too, but with a petite charcoal grill (3), a sturdy side table is a must. Rustic portables (4) have charm, but you'll find one with a vented lid gives more cooking scope; for example, a miniature version (5) of the classic kettle grill (6).

CHOOSING FUELS

The charcoal briquette is so easy to find that it is the default fuel for most grillers. And, although our top choice for fuel is always hardwood charcoal, briquettes are fine with us, too, provided that you give them time for the chemicals they contain to burn off. Hardwood logs (*see p24*) are ideal for those who love tinkering with a fire, but their unpredictability can be challenging. One of our favourite fire-building techniques is to combine charcoal with a single log (*see p30*). That way, you get the best of both fuels. Finally, of course, there's gas (*see p25*): we have to say that for us, it will never rival the joys of live-fire cooking, but there's no denying its convenience.

FUEL YOUR IMAGINATION Logs appeal to those who crave a truly primal grilling experience, but traditional hardwood charcoal also has a long and distinguished history in firebuilding.

THE REAL DEAL Hardwood charcoal certainly gives a superior grilling experience. If you can find a supplier whose charcoal comes from sustainable sources, you can feel good about that, too.

THE UBIQUITOUS BRIQUETTE These familiar little pillow shapes can be bought almost anywhere. Cheap, clean, and convenient, they can provide a good, even, and intense heat.

HARDWOOD CHARCOAL

This is the real deal, charcoal made by the traditional method, which involves burning hardwood in a closed container with very little oxygen. Because it is simply wood that has been reduced to charcoal, it comes in irregularly-shaped lumps rather than uniform briquettes. It has several advantages over briquettes, all of which derive from the fact that it is almost pure carbon – it lights a little more easily, it is more responsive to changes in oxygen level so you can regulate it more easily, and (most importantly) it burns cleaner and hotter than briquettes. Its major disadvantage is that it's more difficult to locate, plus it is slightly more expensive.

CHARCOAL BRIQUETTES

Briquettes have several advantages: You can find them anywhere, they provide a good, hot fire if you use enough of them, and they are relatively inexpensive. They do have one disadvantage, though – they are not pure charcoal. Instead, they are powdered charcoal pressed together with binders, and sometimes chemical additives so they will light more easily. The only real problem with this is that until the briquettes are completely caught, a little bit of what you are burning is chemicals. So when you use briquettes, just be sure that you don't put any food over them until all the briquettes are totally covered with grey ash.

LOG FIRE Though the heat they provide is unpredictable, logs are great fun to grill over. A single log combined with a charcoal fire, however, gives you the best of both worlds.

HERB BRANCHES Cut your own for an inexpensive way to create a Mediterranean atmosphere – but unless you're doing lid-on cookery, they won't add much flavour to the food.

HARDWOOD LOGS

Logs are, of course, the original grilling fuel. Their primary characteristics are that they burn for a long time, which is a good thing, and that they burn unevenly and unpredictably, which can be either good or bad. If you're one of those people who think tending the fire is fun, then this is the fuel for you, because there's a lot of watching and shifting around involved. We like to compromise with a "dual fuel" fire (*see* Our Favourite Fire, *p30*). It's best to use seasoned logs. Greenwood chunks and chips are great for adding a little extra aroma (*see right*), but a greenwood fire will spit and smoke too much for good grilling.

MINOR FUEL OPTIONS

Wood chips and other aromatics such as vine trimmings and dried herbs are appropriate for slower, covered techniques such as smoke-roasting or barbecuing. In those situations, the food is going to spend enough time bathed in the smoke to pick up some of its flavour characteristics. (You can even use chunky trimmings from hardwood trees in your garden, such as apple and maple; the greener they are, the more smoke they will produce.) When you are doing just straight grilling, however, all they really do is perfume the air, not the food. So unless you're a big believer in aromatherapy, save these aromatics for covered cooking.

GRILLING ON GAS

The advice we've given so far, of course, all relates to charcoal grills. But let's talk for a minute about gas grills. We don't have a lot to say about them, because we don't have much experience with them. The reason is simple: we love the excitement and unpredictability of live fire, so we really don't use gas. But their speed and convenience have made gas grills increasingly popular and, while you won't get the same experience as with true live fire, it's certainly a lot better than not grilling at all.

COOKING ON A GAS GRILL

Any of the recipes in this book can easily be done over a gas grill. Just be sure that you let the grill heat up for 15 minutes (with the lid closed) before you begin to cook, and set the dial to hot, medium, or low. When we call for a "multilevel fire", turn off the burner on one side or at the front or back, depending upon how your grill is configured.

A lid is essential to build up a good grilling temperature

A generous grill area is our number one requirement, whatever the fuel

Check that the grill base slopes for good drainage to minimize flare-ups

The more you spend, the more extra features for convenience you'll get, such as these wings

CHOOSING A GAS GRILL

Follow the same general rules as with a charcoal grill (*see p20*) – get the biggest and most powerful one you can afford and accommodate, so you'll have room to cook a lot at the same time, and get some char on your food.

Dual burners give you two temperature zones that mimic a multilevel live fire

The gas bottle will usually be enclosed or screened. Make sure there's a gauge that tells you how much fuel you have left

ESSENTIAL GRILLING TOOLS

HAVING THE RIGHT TOOLS makes any task easier, and that's true of grilling, as well. The trick is to have all the tools you actually need without cluttering up your grill with a lot of unnecessary stuff. Here's our essential list. **1. HEAVY-DUTY, LONG-HANDLED, SPRING-LOADED TONGS** The number one grill tool. Like an extra hand that doesn't get burned, they are ideal for placing food on the grill, moving it around while it's cooking, picking it up to check for doneness, and taking it off the grill. Get two or three, so you can place them strategically around the grilling area. Each qualifier is important: the tongs should be heavy-duty so they will not bend when you lift big pieces of food; have long handles so you can work over a hot fire without burning your arms; and be spring-loaded so they are always ready to use, rather than having to be opened each time. **2. WIRE BRUSH** The brushes that come with fancy grill sets are usually not as sturdy or efficient as the ones for paint-scraping that you pick up at a hardware store. They're great for cleaning the grill grid right after you finish cooking, before any grease congeals and while the hot coals will disintegrate any food residue that falls into them. This brush will be your biggest ally in the war against sticking. Since they do wear out, pick up a couple – preferably the wooden-handled variety, which are more durable. **3. DISPOSABLE FOIL TRAYS** These might seem an odd essential, but they have many uses. They're just the thing for carrying raw food to the grill and cooked food from grill to table. They're also ideal for covering that big, thick pork chop or bone-in chicken breast that's not quite done yet but has to stay on the cooler side of the fire to finish cooking; it allows you to create a kind of mini-oven without closing the grill lid and trapping ashy, "off" flavours. **4. THERMOMETERS** We like to keep two types

handy: a small, dial-face, instant-read thermometer for checking the interior doneness of roasts, chickens, or anything else big and bulky, and an oven thermometer to put inside the grill if it doesn't have one and you're going to smoke-roast or barbecue. **5. DOG-LEG SPATULA** Much as we like tongs, there are some things – delicate fish fillets, for example – better lifted or turned with a dog-leg or offset spatula with a large surface area. The dog-leg feature lets you slip the blade under the food more easily, and the large surface area is important so that foods don't hang off the edges and break. **6. INEXPENSIVE TEA TOWELS** Use them to pick up hot dishes or skewers – it's much quicker to grab a couple of cloths than to fit your hand into a mitt. Just be sure they're not wet when you use them this way, since wet cloth is a great heat conductor. Of course, they also come in handy for spills and generally keeping your grilling environment neat. **7. SKEWERS** You'll need these for kebabs, of course, and they can be useful for small items, since threading them onto skewers keeps them from falling through the grill grid. Some folks like metal skewers because they can be reused; others prefer the convenience of disposable wooden ones. If you go with the latter, don't bother soaking them before using them; the portion of the skewer inside the food isn't going to burn, and the part outside the food will dry and burn over the fire, anyway. **8. YOUR FAVOURITE BEVERAGE** Next to tongs, this may be the most indispensable grilling tool. It helps keep you cool and calm while you're tending the fire – a key to success. It also helps you keep your perspective – remember that the point of grilling is not just to cook delicious food, but also to have fun. When you're having fun, so will your guests, which means that even if something isn't cooked perfectly, dinner will still be a success. Since you don't want to be running inside to get a refill, we recommend having an ice bucket filled with Favourite Beverage right by your side. That way, you can also graciously share with guests.

BUILDING THE FIRE

You can either lay a very simple fire, basically consisting of a pile of charcoal, or a slightly more complicated, multilevel type; it all depends on what you are cooking. Use plenty of charcoal when building your fire. After all, you're spending more on the food than on the fuel, and having a fire that is large enough and hot enough is a key to good grilling.

SIMPLE ONE-LEVEL FIRE

If you are cooking something small that is easily cooked through on the inside without burning on the outside, such as a steak or a boneless chicken breast, you want to cook it directly above the coals. In that case, you can build a one-level fire, simply following the instructions on pp32–3 for lighting your fuel. We do recommend, however, that even when building this very elemental fire you leave a space in the grill bed with no coals.

OUR FAVOURITE FIRE

To add a little more grilling scope to a simple fire, our very favourite technique is to shore up the charcoal with a small log. Once the coals are completely lit, position the log along the edge of the coals and use your tongs to push it across the bottom of the grill, bunching the coals up behind it. Once it catches, you'll get both the steady, predictable heat of the charcoal and the long-lasting, smoky heat of the wood.

A "dead area" with no coals gives you a place to move food to in case of flare-ups (*see p34*)

A log along the edge of your charcoal helps keep the fire going and gives smoky flavour

A MULTILEVEL FIRE gives you control when cooking something like a thick steak, where the relationship between surface sear and interior doneness needs to be finely balanced.

A GOOD-SIZED GRILL makes it far easier to lay a generous multilevel fire; the different grilling zones then allow you to cook a variety of items that need different cooking temperatures.

MULTILEVEL CHARCOAL FIRE

If you are cooking something such as a thick pork chop or a bone-in chicken breast, you need a multilevel fire. The reason is quite straightforward: if you have a fire with hotter and cooler portions, you can move food around according to whether it needs more sear on the outside (to the hot zone) or more cooking on the inside without exterior sear (to the cool zone). Laying this fire is only slightly more complicated. To do so, lay a bed of charcoal that is about 7.5cm (3in) deep on one side, tapers out to about 2.5cm (1in) on the other side, and is larger in surface area than the total surface area of the food you are planning to grill. This way, you will end up with a very hot side and a cooler side. As an alternative, you can initially build the fire in one side of the grill, then shove some of the coals over to the other side after the fire is well-lit. To our way of thinking, it is so simple to lay a multilevel

fire that you might as well do it as a matter of course, on the chance that you will need the various levels of heat. However, in those recipes where you are doing direct grilling only, we do not call for this. You decide.

A thick bed of coals gives fierce heat at the back, tapering to a single layer of coals for more gentle heat

STARTING THE FIRE

USING A CHIMNEY STARTER

The best tool for lighting a fire, in our opinion, is the chimney starter. It's an incredibly simple device consisting of a sheet metal cylinder, open at both ends, with a ring of ventilation holes around the bottom, a grid located inside the flue a little way up from the bottom, and a handle. To use it, you just set it in the middle of the fire grate, fill the bottom section with crumpled newspaper, then fill the top with charcoal and light the newspaper. The flames will sweep up through the chimney, igniting the charcoal. When the charcoal is red-hot, which should take about five minutes, dump it out and put as much additional charcoal as you want on top of or around it. It's that quick and easy.

OTHER OPTIONS

Of course, there are other options for starting your fire. Lighter fluid, which has acquired a tarnished reputation lately, is actually an acceptable choice, provided that you wait until the coals are all lit before you start cooking (which you should do, anyway). Another reasonable option is the electric coil starter, which consists of a thick, oval electrical coil with a plastic handle. You

FIRELIGHTING METHODS

CHIMNEY STARTER Also known as a flue, this is one of those wonderful tools that is simple yet 100% effective. You just light the paper at the base – the flames are then drawn up to ignite the coals.

LIGHTER FLUID This has been criticized for imparting chemical flavours, but if you wait until the fluid is all burned off before you put anything over the fire, it won't affect the food.

ELECTRIC STARTER Once the red-hot electric element ignites the charcoal resting on it, unplug the starter and set it aside on a fireproof surface, out of reach of children, until it is cool.

WAITING TO COOK Just a few lit coals will ignite the rest; then, wait for the flames to die down. As white ash starts to cover the charcoal, the temperature will rise until all the coals are grey.

put it right on the grate, mound charcoal on top of it, and plug it into an earthed socket; the coil will soon become red-hot, igniting the charcoal that's in contact with it.

ONCE THE FIRE IS LIT

Remember, there's no need to light all the charcoal with your starting method. As long as you get at least one piece of charcoal going, it will light the piece of charcoal next to it, which will light the ones next to it, and so on. It will take 20–30 minutes for the fire to work up to the fiery-red stage, then die down until the coals become covered with a fine, grey ash. Then, once the fire reaches the correct temperature for your food (*see overleaf*), you're ready to cook.

MANAGING YOUR FIRE

GAUGING THE TEMPERATURE

Wait until the coals are completely covered with grey ash, then hold your hand 12cm (5in) above the grill grid. Count how many seconds you can comfortably leave it there.
1–2 seconds The fire is **hot**;
3–4 seconds You have **medium** heat;
5–6 seconds You have a **low** fire.
The fire's heat will peak when all the coals are grey, then slowly start to cool down, so start checking the temperature early. If you miss the peak of heat and need a hot fire, add more coals and wait until they are all grey.

ALL OUR GRILL RECIPES specify either a hot, medium, or low grilling heat, so to ensure success, it's important to check the fire's temperature before you put the food on the grill.

DEALING WITH FLARE-UPS

Many people will tell you that the way to deal with flare-ups is to have a squirt bottle of water handy to douse the offending flames. This is wrong. What happens when you do this is that you raise a plume of ash, which gets on the food you're cooking. Instead, when flare-ups occur – as they inevitably will when you are cooking any fatty food directly over the coals – simply move the food to the section of the grill with no coals, wait for the flare-up to die down, and then put the food back over the coals.

FLARE-UPS ARE CAUSED when fat drips onto the hot coals. Take away the cause of the problem by moving the food over to the "dead area" of the grill, and the flames will quickly die down.

TAKE OUR ADVICE and cover the grill only when you're doing indirect-heat grilling, like barbecuing and smoke-roasting, where the food isn't directly over the coals.

BE PREPARED for emergencies; although you may never need it, having something to hand with which to douse the fire will give you peace of mind whenever you grill.

USING THE LID

Be sure you use the grill cover correctly. What this means – despite what most manufacturers tell you – is that you should cover the grill only when you are doing long, indirect cooking, never when you are cooking directly over the coals. When food is right over the coals, fat tends to drip into the fire, where it is transformed into rather acrid smoke. When the grill is uncovered, this smoke dissipates; with the grill covered, though, the food is bathed in that unpleasant smoke. It's not harmful, but it does give the food a distinct "off" flavour. When you are smoke-roasting, there is no fat dripping into the coals, and in any case the food spends long enough in contact with smoke from the charcoal to overcome any off flavour.

STAYING SAFE

Grilling is fun and you want to be relaxed when you're doing it, but you still need to pay attention to safety. After all, this is live fire. So always set up your grill on level ground in the largest possible open space, away from walls, fences, overhanging eaves or tree branches, or anything else that might easily catch fire. Never light a fire with petrol, and never spray lighter fluid onto lit coals. We always have a fire extinguisher handy when we're grilling (although we keep it discreetly out of sight). If you don't have one, have a garden hose or bucket of sand nearby. Don't let kids or dogs run or play in the grilling area. And finally, always close down your grill, including the vents, after you are done with a grilling session.

KNOWING WHEN FOOD IS DONE

Since each live fire is a bit different from all others, the cooking times we give in recipes are really just estimates based on our experience. This means that judging the doneness of food is perhaps the most important skill a grill cook can possess. Whichever method you use (*see opposite*), testing for yourself is of crucial importance, and we recommend that you do it early and often. Remember that there is only a relatively small window of perfect doneness, and you need to catch the food at that point.

IS IT DONE YET?

Whichever method you use to check for doneness, remember that the food will keep cooking for a while after it is removed from the heat (this is called "carryover cooking").

• Take that **steak** off when the degree of doneness is one less than you like it; when it looks rare if you really want it medium-rare, for example. The same goes for thick **chops** and juicy **roasts** of red meats.

• Remove **fish** from the flames when it still has a trace of translucency in the middle, since your ultimate aim is a fish (or **prawn**) that is just barely opaque in the centre.

• When it comes to **chicken**, though, ignore the rules above: leave it on the fire until it is completely opaque all the way through and there is no pink at all in the centre or, especially, down near the bone.

CARRYOVER COOKING Start checking for doneness well before you think the food is ready to come off the grill; it will continue to cook after it comes off the flames. If the recipe recommends letting meat rest, inverting a foil tray over it, or tenting it with foil, will keep it warm as it sits.

1. THE "HAND METHOD"

As protein cooks, it becomes increasingly firm. Experienced cooks can judge the degree of doneness of a piece of meat (or fowl or fish) simply by pushing on it with a finger. The firmer it is, the more done it is. Young cooks are taught that rare corresponds to the fleshy area (A) between the thumb and forefinger, for example, while well-done feels like the base of the thumb (B). This method does require a lot of practice. That doesn't mean it's not worth learning, it just means backing it up while you learn.

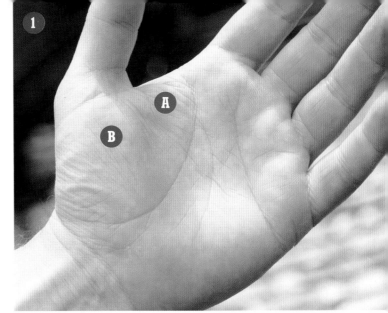

2. "NICK AND PEEK" METHOD

Totally practical, totally reliable: as the name implies, you simply pick up one of whatever you are cooking, nick it slightly with a knife so you can look inside, and check its state of doneness. That's all there is to it. You couldn't get much easier or more accurate. And don't worry about losing a lot of juice by cutting into the food; the very small amount of juice you may lose pales in comparison to serving raw or burned food.

3. A MEAT THERMOMETER

For large cuts of meat or whole fowl – basically anything that you grill-roast – the best option is to check the internal temperature. With a roast, you want to poke the thermometer all the way through to the other side of the meat, then draw it back to the mid-point to get a reading. When checking the doneness of a whole bird, insert the thermometer at an angle into the area between the drumstick and the breast, looking to hit the thickest part of the thigh.

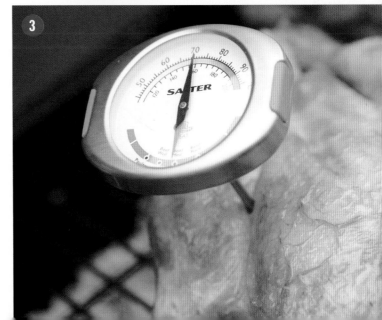

ENHANCING FLAVOURS

The unique, supremely delicious taste of grilled food is a perfect vehicle for a wide range of flavour enhancers. From chillies, herbs, and spices used individually, to spice pastes and rubs to glazes and an astonishing variety of relishes, salsas, chutneys, sambals – not to mention traditional barbecue sauces – the grilling world is a world of deep flavour. And, of course, any grilled food is enhanced by the proper use of salt and pepper.

SALT

Add the right amount of salt to a dish, and all the other flavours open up, blend more harmoniously, and become fuller on the tongue. In other words, it tastes better. In our experience, most folks tend to use too little salt. Be a little more generous than you think you should, and you'll likely find your cooking improves. Our preference is for kosher rather than table salt. Coarse sea salt is another good alternative. It has no additives, and its large crystals make it easier to judge just how much salt you're adding when you use your fingers – the best way to do it.

PEPPER

When it comes to pepper, there is no substitute for fresh ground, which has ten times the flavour of pre-ground. We prefer to grind coarsely so the large chunks explode with flavour and heat in your mouth when you bite into them. As with salt, use it generously. For small amounts, a standard pepper grinder is fine. When you need more than a few tablespoons, you can either crack the peppercorns by rolling a heavy sauté pan back and forth over them while bearing down on the pan, or pulse them three or four times in a clean electric coffee grinder.

HERBS

The fresh, verdant flavours and aromatics that herbs add to food can't be beat. We sometimes use the dried option when it is traditional in a certain type of dish, but are more likely to go for fresh herbs, since they are more vibrant. We particularly like to toss them into dishes at the end of cooking, an easy way of adding a spark of flavour. We're also very fond of the lovely Southeast Asian tradition of using fresh herbs as greens.

CHILLIES

Perhaps the most thrilling of all flavourings, chilli peppers bring not only heat, but also complex character to all kinds of dishes. However, their seemingly endless variety can be bewildering. If you're a true chilli-head, then go ahead and experiment with every last one. Otherwise, we suggest you select a type that is readily available where you live, get to know it well, and feel free to use it anywhere we call for chillies in this book.

SPICES

Spices are a large part of what makes everyday food exciting. In fact, one of the things we like best about grilled food is that it has the character to stand up to the intensity of spices. If you can, it's best to buy spices whole and grind them yourself, which increases their depth of flavour exponentially. If you do buy spices pre-ground, don't hold on to them too long, since their flavour fades markedly after a few months. We often toast spices – especially cumin and coriander – which gently brings out a whole new dimension of fragrance.

WHEN TO FLAVOUR FOOD

We like to salt food before it goes on the fire. Some experts say you should avoid this because it draws moisture out of the food. But we think this is more than compensated for by the fact that the salt has a chance to interact with the food and amplify its flavours. When it comes to adding other flavourings before cooking, we prefer spice rubs and pastes to marinades because they give more intense flavour and can be used at the last minute. We also like to glaze food while it's on the grill – the sweet stickiness this imparts is especially suited to cuts of pork and poultry. And we rarely grill without serving a home-made accompaniment to the main dish – spicy or fragrant, fiery or cooling – so that our guests can help themselves to yet more flavour.

PREPARING YOUR OWN spice mixtures and relishes ensures that flavours are always super-fresh, clean, and lively.

A DRY SPICE MIXTURE can be bound together with olive oil or vegetable oil to form a paste that adheres well to food.

SPICE RUBS AND PASTES

The quickest and most effective way to add wonderfully intense flavours to grilled food is to coat it with a blend of spices before it goes on the grill. Whether dry (spice rubs) or wet (spice pastes), these mixtures work wonderfully well, since the high heat of the fire transforms them into hyper-flavourful crusts on the exterior of the food. Also, they can be made in advance, so all you have to do at the last minute is rub them on and you're ready to cook. Keep a supply of your favourite rub or mix handy, and you'll always be ready for a great grilled dinner.

AN ORDINARY PAINTBRUSH works better and lasts longer than a cook's pastry brush in the robust world of grilling.

TRADITIONAL SEASONINGS such as mustard can be opened up by the addition of dried fruits such as apricots.

GLAZES

Who doesn't love food with a glistening, slightly sticky, sweetly flavourful glaze? Be careful, though, to add these flavourful coatings only during the last few minutes that the food is over the coals. Most glazes contain a sweetener − either in the form of sugar itself or in some other ingredient such as orange juice, honey, molasses, or redcurrant jelly − so if you put the glaze on too early, these sugars will burn rather than properly caramelising. As a bonus, surplus glaze mixture can be passed round as a sauce when you serve up the main dish.

ACCOMPANIMENTS

In traditional European cuisines, dishes are often accompanied with sauces created by deglazing what's left in the pan after the meat or fish is cooked. This is not possible with grilling, since there's no pan involved. But cooks in tropical climates, where grilling is the most common cooking method, have created a wide array of fruit and vegetable mixtures to accompany grilled food. Called by various names – salsas, chutneys, sambals, blatjangs, relishes – these inventive accompaniments bring a wealth of pungent, aromatic flavours to the table.

STEAKS, CHOPS, AND RIBS

FIRE AND MEAT WERE MADE FOR EACH OTHER. AND HERE YOU'VE GOT IT ALL, FROM PRIMAL STEAKS TO SUCCULENT RIBS – EVERY KIND OF RED MEAT, WITH RUBS AND PASTES AND RELISHES TO MAKE THEM EVEN MORE FLAVOURFUL. THIS IS WHAT GRILLING IS ALL ABOUT.

PEPPERED RIBEYE STEAK
WITH BLUE CHEESE-PECAN BUTTER

To us, the ribeye is the king of steaks, with the perfect combination of flavour and tenderness. A thick coating of freshly cracked black pepper, a little sprinkling of chilli pepper flakes, and a knob of butter enriched with blue cheese and toasted pecans is our favourite way of gilding this particular lily.

Serves 4

THE MEAT

60g (2oz) freshly cracked black pepper
60g (2oz) kosher salt
1 tbsp chilli pepper flakes
4 boneless ribeye steaks, each 350–400g (12–14oz) and about 2.5cm (1in) thick
2 tbsp olive oil

THE BUTTER

1 tbsp chopped pecan nuts
60g (2oz) unsalted butter, softened
60g (2oz) crumbled blue cheese
1 tsp fresh lemon juice

Toast the pecans: heat the oven to 180°C (350°F/Gas 4), spread the pecans over a shallow baking pan, and cook, checking frequently, until golden (5–10 minutes). Allow to cool.

Combine the butter, blue cheese, pecans, and lemon juice in a small bowl and mix well. Pile the butter mixture onto a piece of greaseproof paper or cling film, form it into a rough cylinder, and wrap it up. Refrigerate until firm. (This butter will keep in the refrigerator for a week, or frozen for several months.)

Build a fire in your grill. When the coals are all ignited, the flames have died down, and the temperature is hot (see p34), you're ready to cook.

Combine the black pepper, salt, and chilli flakes in a small bowl and mix well. Rub the steaks all over with oil and coat generously with the spice mixture, pressing gently to be sure it adheres.

Put the steaks on the grill over the hottest part of the fire and cook, turning once, until very well seared – about 6–8 minutes per side for rare. To check for doneness, poke the steaks with your finger to test their firmness (see p37); if you're unsure, make a small cut in the thickest part of one steak to be sure it is just slightly less done than you like it.

While the steaks are cooking, cut the chilled blue cheese butter into 5mm (¼in) slices. As soon as the steaks come off the grill, top each steak with a slice or two of the butter, so it starts to melt as you serve the steaks.

CUBAN PORK RIBS
WITH MANGO MOJO

If you've ever travelled in the Latin Caribbean, you know that there are plenty of hardcore grillers down there, and they like to put a little different flavour profile on their ribs than we are used to up north. That's great with us, because we love the way lime, garlic, chillies, and sweet mango match up with the smoky ribs. This also works well using the oven-based "cheater" method found in our Memphis-style rib recipe (*see pp68–9*), since that lets you get a taste of the Caribbean even on days when you can't haul out the grill.

Serves 4–6

THE MEAT

4 tbsp ground annatto (or substitute paprika)
2 tbsp ground cumin
2 tbsp kosher salt
2 tbsp freshly cracked black pepper
2 tbsp finely chopped fresh garlic
2 racks pork spareribs, up to 1.35kg (3lb) each (known as 3.5/down in the trade)
2 tbsp olive oil

THE MOJO

1 ripe mango, peeled, stoned, and diced small
120ml (4fl oz) olive oil
4 tbsp distilled white vinegar
Juice of 2 limes (about 4 tbsp)
4 tbsp roughly chopped fresh coriander
2 tbsp finely chopped fresh chilli pepper of your choice
1 tbsp finely chopped fresh garlic
Kosher salt and freshly cracked black pepper to taste

Light a fire well over to one side of your grill, using enough coals to fill half a shoebox.

Combine the annatto, cumin, salt, pepper, and garlic in a small bowl and mix well. Rub the ribs with the oil, then coat them thoroughly on all sides with the spice mixture, pressing gently to be sure it adheres.

When the coals are well lit, place the ribs on the side of the grill away from the coals, being careful that none of the meat is directly over the coals. Put the lid on the grill with the vents open one-quarter of the way and cook, adding a handful of fresh charcoal about every 30 minutes, until the juice runs clear when you poke the meat with a fork and the meat is tender and pulls easily from the bone (3–4 hours).

While the ribs are cooking, combine the mojo ingredients in a small bowl, mix well, and set aside.

When the meat is done, remove from the grill, cut the racks into individual ribs, and serve "dry", passing the sauce on the side.

GREEK RACK OF LAMB
WITH GRILLED PEPPER SALAD

When we think of grilled lamb, we think of grilled peppers, and when we think of grilled peppers, we think of feta cheese. Here we put it all together by topping rib chops with a mix of grilled peppers, rosemary, feta, lemon, and parsley. You can cut the lamb racks into single chops for refined eaters, or double chops for a more robust meat experience.

Serves 4

THE MEAT

2 racks lamb, 350–400g (12–14oz) each
2 tbsp vegetable oil
Kosher salt and freshly cracked black pepper to taste
3 tbsp roughly chopped fresh rosemary

THE TOPPING

4 tbsp extra virgin olive oil
Juice of 1 lemon (about 4 tbsp)
4 tbsp roughly chopped fresh parsley
115g (4oz) feta cheese, diced small or crumbled
Kosher salt and freshly cracked black pepper to taste
2 red, yellow, or orange peppers, halved lengthways, cored, and deseeded
1 tbsp vegetable oil

Light a fire well over to one side of your grill, using enough coals to fill a large shoebox. When the fire has died down, the coals are covered in white ash, and the temperature is medium (see p34), you're ready to cook.

Rub the lamb racks with the vegetable oil, sprinkle them generously with salt and pepper, and pat all over with the rosemary, pressing gently to be sure it adheres.

Put the racks on the grill, fat side up, over the coals but near the edge of the fire. As soon as the side facing down is nicely browned, which should take about 15 minutes, flip the racks over and cook until the fat side is also well browned – about another 15 minutes. Watch carefully for flare-ups during this time; if they do occur, move the rack to the part of the grill with no coals until the flames have disappeared. To check for doneness, poke one of the racks with your finger to test its firmness (see p37); if you are unsure, insert a meat thermometer into the thickest part of the lamb, let it sit for 5 seconds, then read the temperature: 49°C (120°F) for rare, 52°C (126°F) for medium-rare, which is how we like it; 57°C (134°F) medium, 65°C (150°F) medium-well, and 71°C (160°F) well done. When done to your liking, remove from the grill. Cover loosely with foil, and allow to sit for 10 minutes.

While the lamb is cooking, combine the olive oil, lemon juice, and parsley in a small bowl, and whisk to blend. Add the feta cheese, season with salt and pepper, and set aside.

When the lamb is nearly done, rub the pepper halves with oil, season with salt and pepper, and grill directly over the coals until golden brown but still crisp (2–3 minutes per side). (Don't char them, since they won't be peeled.) When the peppers are done, cut them into (1cm (½in) wide strips, add to the bowl of feta, and toss gently.

Cut the lamb racks into double or single chops, arrange on a serving plate, and spoon the feta-pepper mixture over them.

LATIN PORK CHOPS WITH PEACH-CHILLI SALSA

We prefer spice rubs to marinades because they add more concentrated flavour, they can be put on at the last minute, and they encourage the formation of a nice crust on the outside of whatever you're putting on the grill. Here we rub pork chops with a simple Latin-style spice combination, and accompany them with a fresh salsa fuelled by the chipotle, a chilli that gets the relationship between heat and flavour just right. Try this one in late summer, when you want to add a little something extra to your pork chop repertoire, and peaches are at the height of their flavour.

Serves 4

THE MEAT

4 pork loin chops, bone-in, about 350g (12oz)
    each and 2.5cm (1in) thick
2 tbsp olive oil

THE RUB

1 tbsp ground cumin
1 tbsp ground coriander
1 tbsp chilli powder
Kosher salt and freshly cracked black pepper to taste

THE SALSA

3 ripe but firm peaches, stoned and diced small
4 tbsp red onion, diced small
1 tbsp chipotle peppers in adobo sauce, mashed
Juice of 3 limes (about 5 tbsp)
5 tbsp roughly chopped fresh coriander
Kosher salt and freshly cracked black pepper to taste

Build a fire in your grill. When the coals are all ignited, the flames have died down, and the temperature is medium (*see p34*), you're ready to cook.

While the fire is heating up, combine the ingredients for the spice rub in a small bowl and mix well. Rub the pork chops lightly with oil, then coat them generously with the spice rub. Set the chops aside while you make the salsa.

Make the salsa: combine the peaches, onion, chipotle, lime juice, coriander, and salt and pepper in a medium bowl and mix well. Set aside.

Put the chops on the grill over the coals and cook, turning once, until done to your liking (10–12 minutes per side for medium). To check for doneness, poke the meat with your finger to test its firmness (*see p37*); if you're unsure, cut into the thickest part of one of the chops and peek at the centre to be sure it is just slightly less done than you like it.

Serve the chops hot, and pass the salsa on the side.

SPICY STEAK TACOS WITH ORANGE-CHILLI GLAZE AND LIME-MARINATED AVOCADOS

Skirt steak has got to be one of the most underappreciated cuts of meat in the world. Not only is it incredibly easy to cook; its unique combination of leanness and fat makes it at once tender and flavourful, and it stacks up well against the strong tastes we love, like the Latin flavours that accompany it here. While chilli powder will work just fine in the glaze, we recommend you seek out chipotles for their wonderful smoky heat.

Serves 4

THE MEAT

1kg (2¼lb) trimmed skirt steak, cut into 4 pieces
1 large red onion, peeled and cut into 1cm (½in) thick rounds (keep rings together)
4 tbsp olive oil
4 tbsp cumin seeds
1 tbsp paprika
Kosher salt and freshly cracked black pepper to taste

THE AVOCADOS

2 ripe but firm avocados
Juice of 6 limes (about 180ml/6fl oz)
4 tbsp roughly chopped fresh coriander
Kosher salt and freshly cracked black pepper to taste

THE GLAZE

240ml (8fl oz) fresh orange juice
120ml (4fl oz) distilled white vinegar
1 tbsp tomato purée
1 tbsp finely chopped chipotle chillies, or 1 tbsp chilli powder

THE WRAPS

12 corn tortillas, 15–20cm (6–8in) diameter

Combine the orange juice, vinegar, tomato purée, and chipotles or chilli powder in a medium saucepan and, on the hob, bring to the boil over a high heat. Reduce the heat to medium and simmer vigorously until the mixture has reduced by two-thirds and become slightly syrupy (30–40 minutes). Remove the glaze from the heat and allow to cool to room temperature.

While the glaze reduces, halve, stone, and peel the avocados; cut each half into thin slices. Put the avocado slices, lime juice, and coriander in a bowl, and sprinkle with salt and pepper. Toss gently until the avocado is evenly coated, then transfer to a serving dish, cover, and set aside until serving time.

Build a fire in your grill. When the coals are all ignited, the flames have died down, and the temperature is hot (*see p34*), you're ready to cook.

Rub the steaks and onion slices with olive oil and sprinkle evenly with the cumin, paprika, and salt and pepper.

When the fire is ready, put the steaks on the grill directly over the coals and cook until they are done to your liking (4–5 minutes per side for medium-rare). Brush the steaks generously with the glaze during the last 45 seconds of cooking on each side.

To check for doneness, poke each steak with your finger to test its firmness (*see p37*); if you're unsure, make a cut in the thickest part of one steak and peek at the centre; it should be slightly less done than you like. Transfer the steaks to a cutting board, cover loosely with foil, and allow to rest for 5 minutes. Thinly slice the steak on the diagonal across the grain, arrange the slices on a serving plate, and drizzle with the remaining glaze.

While the steaks rest, put the tortillas around the edges of the grill and cook briefly, flipping every 10 seconds or so, until they are soft and pliable (about 1 minute). Wrap the stack of warm tortillas in a large napkin or foil, and take them to the table along with the lime-marinated avocados and the steak, so your guests can "roll their own".

VEAL CHOPS
WITH GRILLED MUSHROOMS AND PORT

This elegant dish, rich with the deep, silky flavours of veal, mushrooms, butter, and port, is a great one for those times when you want to really pull out all the stops. Since veal is more delicate than beef, you don't want to grill these chops as hard as you would a steak, but the smoky flavour that it gets over the coals still provides a great complement to the tender, subtle meat.

Serves 4

THE MEAT

4 veal rib chops, 350–400g (12–14oz) each, about
    3.5cm (1½in) thick
2 tbsp olive oil
2 tbsp fresh thyme leaves
Kosher salt and freshly cracked black pepper to taste

THE MUSHROOMS

450g (1lb) white mushrooms, cleaned and stems
    trimmed
3 tbsp olive oil
85g (3oz) unsalted butter
4 tbsp port wine
4 tbsp roughly chopped fresh parsley

Build a fire in your grill. When the coals are all ignited, the flames have died down, and the temperature is medium (*see p34*), you're ready to cook.

Rub the chops with the 2 tbsp of olive oil, sprinkle the thyme over them, and season them generously with salt and pepper. Put them over the coals and grill until they are well-seared on the outside and done to your liking inside (8–10 minutes per side for medium). To check for doneness, poke the chops with your finger to test the meat's firmness (*see p37*); if you're unsure, make a small cut and peek inside to be sure the chops are slightly less done than you like them, to allow for carryover cooking. When the chops are done, transfer them to a serving plate, cover them loosely with foil, and allow to rest for about 10 minutes.

While the chops are cooking, put the mushrooms and the 3 tbsp of olive oil in a bowl and toss to coat. Put the mushrooms on the grill beside the chops and cook until they are moist all the way through (about 10 minutes). When the mushrooms are done, remove them from the grill, cut them into quarters, and return them to the bowl you tossed them in. Immediately add the butter, port, and parsley, and mix gently until the butter is melted and the mushrooms are evenly coated. Season with salt and pepper, and cover with foil to keep warm.

Put one chop on each plate, spoon some of the mushrooms on top, and serve.

CURRIED BABY BACK RIBS
WITH INSANELY HOT SCOTCH BONNET SAUCE

The Scotch Bonnet just might be our favourite chilli pepper. Yes, it's very, very hot, but it's a heat backed up with intense, aromatic flavour. Here we match it with a spice rub that features curry powder, widely used in the West Indies where the Scotch Bonnet originated. To shorten the cooking time, we use baby back ribs rather than the full-sized version. Beware – this dish is *really* hot.

Serves 4–6 as an appetizer

THE MEAT

4 tbsp olive oil

4 tbsp freshly cracked coriander seed

2 tbsp curry powder

2 tbsp paprika

1 tbsp brown sugar

2 racks baby back pork ribs, each about 675g (1½lb)

THE SAUCE

6–10 Scotch Bonnet chillies, stemmed, but including seeds and ribs

120ml (4fl oz) fresh orange juice

5 tbsp American yellow mustard

4 tbsp roughly chopped fresh coriander

2 tbsp soft dark brown sugar

Kosher salt and freshly cracked black pepper to taste

Light a fire well over to one side of your grill, using enough coals to fill half a shoebox.

Combine the olive oil, coriander, curry powder, paprika, and brown sugar in a small bowl and mix well. Rub this mixture all over the ribs.

When the flames have died down and the coals are covered in white ash, place the ribs on the side of the grill away from the coals, being careful that none of the meat is directly over the coals. Put the lid on the grill with the vents one-quarter of the way open. Cook the ribs for 30–45 minutes, adding a handful of fresh charcoal after 30 minutes. Turn the ribs over and cook them for 10–20 minutes more. To check for doneness, cut into one of the ribs to be sure that there is no pinkness down near the bone.

While the ribs are cooking, make the sauce: combine the chillies, orange juice, mustard, coriander, and brown sugar in a food processor or blender and purée.

When the ribs are done, brush them with the sauce and cook for about 30 seconds more on each side. Remove the ribs from the grill, cut them apart, and serve, passing any remaining sauce on the side.

PORK TENDERLOINS WITH GREEN CHILLI-SWEETCORN SALSA

Along with Scotch Bonnets, chipotles are our favourite chilli peppers. Their aromatic, smoky, pretty-much-indescribable flavour turns pork tenderloin into a spicy, flavourful luxury. We like chipotles in adobo sauce, although these days you can also find them dried. If you are using the dried ones, be sure to let them sit in boiling-hot water for about 20 minutes first, to plump up and become tender. The chilli-sweetcorn salsa also goes great with just about any other pork dish, from a smoke-roasted loin to a plain grilled chop.

Serves 4

THE MEAT

2 pork tenderloins, about 450g (1lb) each
Kosher salt and freshly cracked black pepper to taste
125g (4½oz) roughly chopped chipotle peppers, preferably canned or bottled in adobo sauce (or substitute dried chipotles, soaked in hot water to reconstitute, and the Adobo Paste recipe on p189)

THE SALSA

2 smallish ears sweetcorn, stripped of husks and silks
2–3 New Mexico or other hot green chillies of your choice, diced small
½ tomato about the size of a tennis ball, cored and diced small
Juice of 2 limes (about 4 tbsp)
2 tbsp roughly chopped fresh coriander
1 tsp ground cumin
Kosher salt and freshly cracked black pepper to taste

Blanch the sweetcorn for the salsa: on the hob, bring a large pan of salted water to the boil, and cook the ears for 1 minute. Drain, and when cool enough to handle, cut the kernels off the cobs.

Build a fire in your grill. When the coals are all ignited, the flames have died down, and the temperature is medium (*see p34*), you're ready to cook.

Sprinkle the tenderloins with salt and pepper, rub them all over with the chipotles and adobo sauce, and place them on the grill directly over the coals. Cook, rolling them around every 3–4 minutes to make sure they cook evenly, until they are done the way you like them (12–15 minutes for medium). To check for doneness, poke the meat with your finger to test its firmness (*see p37*); if you're unsure, cut into the pork at the thickest point to be sure it is slightly less done than you like. Transfer the tenderloins to a serving plate, cover loosely with foil, and allow to rest for 5–10 minutes.

While the pork is resting, combine the sweetcorn kernels with all of the other salsa ingredients in a bowl and mix well. Set aside.

Carve the pork tenderloins crossways into 1cm (½in) thick slices and arrange them on a serving plate. Spoon the salsa over the pork and serve, passing any remaining salsa separately.

ROSEMARY-GRILLED NEW YORK STRIP STEAK WITH CARAMELISED RED ONION JAM

Steak on the grill is the ultimate classic, and for good reason: the rich, deep flavour of beef is perhaps the ideal foil for the smoky char of the grill. This straightforward recipe adds a little aromatic rosemary and garlic to the mix, along with an easy but flavourful onion jam. The jam will last for 10 days, covered and refrigerated, so you might want to make a double batch during high grilling season; it's great with pork and hamburgers as well as steak.

Serves 4

THE MEAT

3 tbsp roughly chopped fresh rosemary
3 tbsp olive oil
1 garlic clove, peeled
1 tbsp kosher salt
1 tbsp freshly cracked black pepper
4 boneless larder-trimmed sirloin steaks*, 350–400g (12–14oz) each and about 3–4cm (1½in) thick

THE ONION JAM

1 head garlic
3 tbsp olive oil, divided
2 medium red onions, peeled and thinly sliced
Kosher salt and freshly cracked black pepper to taste
4 tbsp balsamic vinegar
1 tbsp soft dark brown sugar

For the jam: heat the oven to 150°C (300°F/Gas 2); slice the top quarter off the head of garlic, set it on a sheet of foil and sprinkle with one tbsp of the olive oil, salt, and pepper, then wrap and roast until soft (about 1 hour). Set it aside to cool. On the hob, heat the rest of the olive oil in a large sauté pan or frying pan over a medium heat until it is hot but not smoking. Add the onions, sprinkle with salt and pepper, and sauté until the onions start to soften (about 5 minutes). Reduce the heat to low and continue to cook, stirring often, until the onions are well caramelised (20–30 minutes). Making sure the garlic is cool enough to handle, squeeze the flesh from each clove. Add the garlic to the onions, stirring to incorporate, then add the vinegar and brown sugar and mix well. Continue cooking until the mixture is sticky and thickens slightly (about 2 minutes more). Remove from the heat and set aside.

While the onions are cooking, build a multilevel fire in your grill (*see p31*). When the coals are all ignited, the flames have died down, and the temperature is hot (*see p34*), you're ready to cook.

Combine the rosemary, olive oil, garlic clove, and salt and pepper in a pestle and mortar or small, sturdy bowl and mash to a paste. Dry the steaks with kitchen paper and rub them all over with the seasoning paste. Put the steaks on the grill over the hottest coals and sear them well (4–5 minutes per side). Slide the steaks over to the cooler part of the grill and continue to cook, turning once, until they are done to your liking (10–12 minutes more for rare). To check for doneness, poke the steaks with your finger to test their firmness (*see p37*); if you're unsure, make a small cut in the thickest steak – it should be just slightly less done than you like it. Transfer the steaks to a serving plate and cover loosely with foil. Let them rest for 5–10 minutes before serving with the onion jam.

*Closely cut to include only the boneless sirloin and fillet eye with very little fat

FLAVOUR FOOTPRINT MEXICAN-LATIN

A prime characteristic of Mexican cooking is the expert and varied use of a huge range of chillies, both fresh and dried. This distinguishes it from many other Latin American cuisines, which are not particularly spicy. But most do share a reliance on the herbs coriander (or *culantro,* a local variant) and oregano, the spices cumin and bay, the juice of oranges and limes, and large quantities of garlic, among other ingredients. If you're unfamiliar with the dynamic cuisines of Latin America, the complex flavours of these simple combinations are going to bring you very pleasant surprises.

All-Purpose Latin Spice Rub
Makes about 50g (1¾oz)

The name says it all – you can rub this on just about anything that you are going to put on the grill. Use a pestle and mortar or the base of a heavy frying pan to crack the coriander seeds.

30g (1oz) freshly cracked coriander seeds
15g (½oz) cumin seeds
2 tbsp freshly cracked black pepper
1 tbsp kosher salt

Combine all the ingredients in a small bowl and mix well. Stored in an airtight container and kept in a cool, dark place, this dry rub will last for a month or longer.

Ancho Chilli Paste
Makes about 60g (2oz)

Rub this onto beef or pork just before it goes on the grill, or use it as a kind of quick marinade and let the flavours soak in and combine for up to 4 hours.

20g (¾oz) dried ancho chillies
4 tbsp roughly chopped fresh coriander
4 tbsp olive oil
2 tbsp cumin seeds
Juice of 1 lime (about 2 tbsp)
1 tbsp finely chopped fresh garlic
1 tbsp kosher salt
1 tbsp freshly cracked black pepper

Soak the chillies in enough hot water to cover them for 20 minutes to rehydrate, then drain and combine with all the other ingredients. Purée in a food processor, or use a pestle and mortar to mash to a paste. This paste will keep, covered and refrigerated, for 2–3 days.

Ancho Chilli Paste

Quick Salsa Rojo
Makes about 450ml (15fl oz)

This classic red salsa is very versatile; it goes beautifully with just about any grilled food.

2 ripe tomatoes, cored and diced small
½ small red onion, peeled and diced
4 tbsp roughly chopped fresh coriander
Juice of 2 limes (about 4 tbsp)
1 tbsp chopped fresh green chilli pepper of your choice
1 tsp ground cumin
Kosher salt and freshly cracked black pepper to taste

Combine all the ingredients in a medium bowl and mix well. This is best used the day it is made, but will keep, covered and refrigerated, for 3–4 days.

Molasses-Jalapeño Barbecue Sauce
Makes about 450ml (15fl oz)

This simple sauce makes a perfect last-minute glaze or accompanying dipping sauce for all manner of grilled food.

240ml (8fl oz) tomato ketchup
5 tbsp treacle or molasses
Juice of 3 limes (about 5 tbsp)
5 tbsp roughly chopped fresh coriander
3 tbsp chopped jalapeño or other fresh green chilli pepper of your choice
Kosher salt and freshly cracked black pepper to taste

Combine all the ingredients in a medium bowl and mix well. This sauce will keep, covered and refrigerated, for 3–4 days.

SIGNATURE INGREDIENTS/TOP ROW (LEFT TO RIGHT) Fresh chillies, dried chillies, coriander; **SECOND ROW** Dried coriander, lime, dried oregano; **THIRD ROW** Avocado, annatto seeds, fresh garlic; **BOTTOM ROW** Cumin seeds, bay leaves, orange.

Green Apple-Chipotle Salsa
Makes about 360ml (12fl oz)

We always like to use green apples in Latin salsas. Their crunch and freshness remind us of jicama, a favourite vegetable of Chris's that holds its juicy, crisp texture beautifully when chopped into salads. This chunky combo is best as an accompaniment to pork, fish, or chicken.

2 Granny Smith apples, cored and diced small
½ red onion, peeled and diced small
2 tbsp finely chopped chipotle peppers in adobo sauce
Juice of 1 lime (about 2 tbsp)
2 tbsp roughly chopped fresh coriander
1 tsp ground cumin
Kosher salt and freshly cracked black pepper to taste

Combine all the ingredients in a medium bowl and mix well. This salsa is best served straight away, but will keep, covered and refrigerated, for 2–3 days.

Green Apple-Chipotle Salsa

GLAZED FLANK STEAK

Although we're generally not in favour of "fusion" cooking, occasionally there's some unlikely combination of ingredients that works so well it's worth it. Here's one such instance – the earthy sweetness of the quintessentially American maple syrup works perfectly with a collection of Asian flavours, from salty soy sauce to aromatic sesame oil and ginger. This is a great dish for those times when you want a quick dinner that's anything but routine.

Serves 4

THE MEAT

30g (1oz) freshly cracked white pepper
2 tbsp sesame oil
2 tbsp soy sauce
1 tbsp peeled and finely chopped fresh ginger
Kosher salt to taste
1 flank steak, about 900g (2lb)
4 tbsp roughly chopped spring onions with green tops

THE GLAZE

5 tbsp maple syrup
4 tbsp soy sauce
2 tbsp sesame oil
1 tbsp peeled and finely chopped fresh ginger
3–4 spring onions, chopped (white and green parts)
1 tsp chilli pepper flakes

Build a fire in your grill. When the coals are all ignited, the flames have died down, and the temperature is hot (*see p34*), you're ready to cook.

Combine all the glaze ingredients in a small bowl, mix well, and set aside.

Combine the white pepper, sesame oil, soy sauce, ginger, and salt in another small bowl. Rub this mixture all over the flank steak. Place the steak over the coals, and grill for 5–7 minutes per side for medium-rare, depending on thickness; brush with glaze during the last minute of cooking on each side. To check for doneness, poke the steak with your finger to test its firmness (*see p37*); if you're unsure, make a small cut and peek inside to be sure that it is slightly less done than you like it, to allow for carryover cooking. Set the steak aside to rest for about 10 minutes before carving.

Slice the steak thinly diagonally across the grain. Arrange the slices on a serving plate, drizzle with some of the glaze, and sprinkle with spring onions. Pass any remaining glaze on the side.

KOREAN BEEF RIBS WITH CHILLI COLE SLAW

Grilling short ribs, which is traditional in Korea, is an unusual approach to a cut of meat that's usually braised. It works beautifully, but be sure you use good-quality meat here; gnarly ribs are going to be tough cooked this way, even after marinating. The chilli slaw makes a great accompaniment to any kind of grilled beef, so long as you're a heat-lover.

Serves 4

THE MEAT

1.35kg (3lb) short ribs of beef,
   1cm (½in) thick

THE SLAW

4 tbsp rice wine vinegar
4 tbsp chilli-garlic sauce
1 tbsp granulated sugar
1 tbsp peeled and finely chopped fresh ginger
250g (9oz) shredded Chinese leaves

THE MARINADE

4 tbsp soy sauce
2 tbsp sesame oil
2 tbsp distilled white vinegar
2 tbsp chopped fresh chilli pepper of your choice
2 tbsp chilli pepper flakes
2 tbsp peeled and finely chopped fresh ginger
1 tbsp finely chopped fresh garlic
1 tsp granulated sugar
Kosher salt and freshly cracked black pepper to taste

Place the short ribs in a large bowl. Combine the marinade ingredients in a small bowl and mix well, then pour the mixture over the ribs, turning them to coat. Cover and refrigerate for about 2 hours, turning once or twice.

Meanwhile, combine the vinegar, chilli-garlic sauce, sugar, and ginger in a small bowl and mix well. Put the Chinese leaves in a large bowl and pour just enough of the dressing over them to moisten, tossing to coat. Cover and refrigerate until serving time.

Build a fire in your grill. When the coals are all ignited, the flames have died down, and the temperature is very hot (see p34), you're ready to cook.

Remove the meat from the marinade and pat it dry with kitchen paper. (Reserve the marinade.) Place the ribs on the grill and cook until they are well-seared on one side (about 3 minutes). Turn and continue cooking to the desired doneness – about 3 minutes more for rare – basting with the reserved marinade during the last minute of cooking. To check for doneness, cut into the meat near a bone to be sure it is slightly less done than you like.

When the ribs are done, transfer them to a serving plate, cover loosely with foil, and allow to rest for 5 minutes. Cut the meat between the bones into individual ribs, and serve them hot, accompanied by the chilli cole slaw.

MEMPHIS RIBS

This is for those of you who don't have the patience or the space to make slow-barbecued ribs. Although they only spend a few minutes on the grill (after several hours in the oven), this version is still mighty delicious. In fact, once they're oven-cooked, you can refrigerate them for up to two days before finishing them off on the grill. They are "Memphis-style" because, like the pitmasters of that rib-centric city, we don't put sauce on the meat. Instead, we coat them with our Traditional Barbecue Rub before they get cooked, then pass the sauce separately along with the cooked ribs. That way, the ribs have a nice, crisp, dry crust on the outside, which you can coat with as much sauce as you like.

Serves 4–6

THE MEAT

2 racks pork spareribs, up to 1.35kg (3lb) each

THE SAUCE

240ml (8fl oz) tomato ketchup
5 tbsp cider vinegar
4 tbsp soft dark brown sugar
4 tbsp orange juice
2 tbsp made brown mustard
½ tsp "liquid smoke" (optional)
Kosher salt and freshly cracked black pepper to taste

TRADITIONAL BARBECUE RUB

5 tbsp kosher salt
5 tbsp freshly cracked black pepper
4 tbsp soft dark brown sugar
2 tbsp paprika
2 tbsp chilli powder
2 tbsp ground cumin
2 tbsp ground coriander
2 tbsp cayenne pepper
1 tbsp ground ginger

In a small bowl, combine all the rub ingredients and mix well. (If you want to multiply the quantities, this mixture will keep, covered and stored in a cool, dry place, for months; it's great with any pork cut or with chicken.)

Preheat the oven to 100°C (200°F/Gas ¼). Coat the ribs thoroughly with the barbecue rub, set them on baking sheets, and roast until the meat is tender and pulls easily from the bone (about 3 hours). Remove the ribs from the oven.

While the ribs are cooking, combine the sauce ingredients in a small bowl, mix well, and set aside.

When the ribs are nearly done, light a small fire in your grill. You want a very low charcoal fire with the grill rack set as high as possible. When the ribs are done, put them on the grill for as long as your patience allows – at least until a light crust has formed, which can take from 10 to 20 minutes per side, depending on your fire. Of course, the longer the ribs cook, the better. Brush them with sauce during the last minute of cooking.

Cut the racks into individual ribs and serve, passing the remaining sauce on the side.

SPICY LAMB SHOULDER CHOPS
WITH CHILLI-GRILLED AVOCADOS

We are big fans of lamb shoulder chops. Although less tender than the more commonly used rib chops, they have deeper lamb flavour and are much less expensive. They are also robust enough to stand up to the dynamic Southwestern flavours we pair them with here. And, if you have never had grilled avocados before, you are in for a big treat.

Serves 4

THE MEAT

8 lamb shoulder chops, about 175g (6oz) each
2 tbsp olive oil
2 tbsp ground cumin
1 tbsp finely chopped fresh garlic
Kosher salt and freshly cracked black pepper to taste

THE AVOCADOS

2 ripe avocados, halved and stoned
2 tbsp olive oil
2 tbsp chilli powder
Kosher salt and freshly cracked black pepper to taste

THE VINAIGRETTE

120ml (4fl oz) olive oil
Juice of 2 limes (about 4 tbsp)
3 tbsp chopped fresh coriander
2 tbsp finely chopped chipotle peppers in adobo sauce
1 tbsp made brown mustard
1 tsp finely chopped fresh garlic
Kosher salt and freshly cracked black pepper to taste

Build a fire in your grill. When the coals are all ignited, the flames have died down, and the temperature is medium-hot (*see p34*), you're ready to cook.

Combine all the vinaigrette ingredients in a small bowl, mix well, and set aside.

Rub the chops lightly with the olive oil, then rub them all over with the cumin, sprinkle them with the garlic, and season generously with salt and pepper. Place on the grill and cook until they are done to your liking (4–5 minutes per side for medium-rare). To check for doneness, poke the chops with your finger to test their firmness (*see p37*); if you're unsure, make a small cut in one chop to be sure that it is slightly less done than you like it. When the chops are done, transfer them to a serving plate, cover loosely with foil, and allow them to rest for about 10 minutes.

While the chops are resting, rub the cut sides of the avocado halves with oil and sprinkle them generously with chilli powder and salt and pepper. Place them cut-side down on the grill and cook until they are golden-brown and slightly charred (3–5 minutes). Arrange the cooked avocados cut-side up around the chops on the serving plate. Stir the vinaigrette to blend and drizzle it generously over everything.

ARGENTINA: IN THE LAND OF BEEF

Driving back to Buenos Aires after a few days out in the immense grasslands known as the pampas, we spied the telltale sign: racks of meat splayed out on a metal stand slanted over a smouldering wood fire.

Braking our little power-deprived car, we swerved into the driveway of the shed behind the fire pit, noting with approval that the restaurant had no name, just a sign outside that said "Domingo-Asado" — "Sunday-Barbecue". Everybody has heard that Argentina is all about beef, but until you see it for yourself, it's hard to believe. On every street corner in every city, it seems, you'll find a *parillada* serving delicious grass-fed beef, most at bargain prices. But the apotheosis of the Argentine beef experience is the *asado*, a cultural ritual born on the pampas. There the cowboys known as gauchos developed a celebratory event in which they slaughtered a cow in the morning, then slowly cooked every bit of it over a wood fire, eating the various cuts as they were done. Like barbecue in the American South or cassoulet in Provence, *asado* is more than just a dish; it is a badge of cultural identity. And the meal we ate in that little shed outside Buenos Aires still followed the formalised sequence. First came a platter of "organ meats" — rich sweetbreads, slightly chewy intestines, fatty chorizo sausage, thick blood sausages — with the obligatory bowl of *chimichurri* sauce. Then, along with a bottle of Malbec wine, a plate of more substantial fare: short ribs, skirt steak, and what the French call entrecôte. At this point we were sated, but we bravely tackled the final wooden platter, this one bearing a giant T-bone and a slab of rump steak. We practically crawled away from the table, but we were satisfied that we had experienced the heart of Argentine cooking.

GIANT T-BONE STEAKS
WITH GREEN PARSLEY SALSA

The classic American steak, T-bone combines a bit of the tenderloin and a bit of the loin. Complementing its full, beefy flavour is a sauce inspired by the *chimichurri* that is a table staple in Argentina and Uruguay, those bastions of beef. The sauce's combination of heat, acidity, and herbaceousness sets off the meat perfectly without overwhelming it. This dish has become a mainstay of Saturday nights at the East Coast Grill, when Executive Chef Eric Gburski brings out the awesome steaks.

Serves 4

2 large (at least 675g/1½lb) T-bone steaks, each 3–4cm (1½in) thick
2 tbsp olive oil
5 tbsp freshly cracked black pepper
4 tbsp kosher salt

For the sauce:
5 tbsp roughly chopped fresh parsley leaves
½ small red onion, peeled and finely chopped
5 tbsp extra virgin olive oil
Juice of 1 lemon (about 4 tbsp)
4 tbsp balsamic vinegar
2 tsp chilli pepper flakes (optional)
Kosher salt and freshly cracked black pepper to taste

Build a multilevel fire (*see p31*) in your grill. When the coals are all ignited, the flames have died down, and the temperature is hot (*see p34*), you're ready to cook.

Rub the steaks all over with oil and coat them generously with pepper and salt, pressing gently to be sure it adheres.

Put the steaks on the grill over the hottest part of the fire and cook, turning once, until well-seared (6–8 minutes per side). Move the steaks to the cooler side of the grill, cover them with a metal pie tin or disposable foil tray, and let them cook slowly until they are done to your liking (8–10 minutes more per side for rare). To check for doneness, poke the steaks with your finger to test their firmness (*see p37*); if you're unsure, make a small cut in the thickest part of one steak to be sure it is just slightly less done inside than you like it.

While the steaks are cooking, combine the sauce ingredients in a bowl and whisk until well-blended.

When the steaks are ready, carve them into thick strips, arrange them on a serving plate, drizzle generously with the sauce, and pass the remaining sauce on the side.

GRILLED LAMB MEDALLIONS WITH ROASTED PEPPER AND BLACK OLIVE RELISH

Saddle of lamb is a great cut of meat, tender but with plenty of lamb flavour. Here we cut it into medallions, sprinkle it with coriander and fennel seeds to accent its slightly aromatic nature, and put it over the coals for just a few minutes. Served with a rather earthy, slightly sharp relish, it's one of our new favourite lamb dishes. If you already have a fire going, you can grill fresh red peppers for the relish (*for method see p78*), but using bottled ones from the kitchen cupboard makes this a really fast and simple dish to prepare.

Serves 4

THE MEAT

4 tbsp freshly cracked black pepper

4 tbsp kosher salt

1 tbsp coriander seeds, freshly cracked

1 tbsp fennel seeds, freshly cracked

900g–1kg (2–2¼lb) boneless saddle of lamb, cut into 2.5cm (1in) thick medallions

2 tbsp olive oil

THE RELISH

225g (8oz) diced roasted red peppers, bottled or home-made

60g (2oz) brine-cured black olives, such as kalamata, pitted and roughly chopped

4 tbsp roughly chopped fresh basil

4 tbsp extra virgin olive oil

4 tbsp balsamic vinegar

1 tbsp finely chopped fresh garlic

Kosher salt and freshly cracked black pepper to taste

Build a fire in your grill. When the coals are all ignited, the flames have died down, and the temperature is medium-hot (*see p34*), you're ready to cook.

Combine the relish ingredients in a small bowl and mix well.

Combine the black pepper, salt, coriander, and fennel in a small bowl and mix well. Rub the lamb with oil and coat it generously with the spice mixture, pressing gently to be sure it adheres. Put the medallions on the grill directly over the coals and cook until they are slightly less done than you like them (6–8 minutes per side for rare). To check for doneness, press the meat with your finger to test its firmness (*see p37*), or make a cut into one medallion and peek inside to check that it is slightly less done than you like it.

Arrange the medallions on a serving plate, top each with a spoonful of relish, and pass the remaining relish on the side.

GRILLED LAMB CHOPS WITH ROASTED RED PEPPER-WALNUT RELISH

The incredible aroma of lamb cooking over an open fire always has two effects on us: it evokes memories of those parts of the world where lamb is king, particularly North Africa, Greece, and Turkey; and it makes us very hungry. The relish that accompanies the lamb chops here – rich with roasted peppers and nuts, with the aroma of mint and the sweet-tart bite of pomegranate molasses – is our homage to the Turkish classic *muhammara*. Although there is truly no substitute for pomegranate molasses, if you can't find it you can use equal parts molasses or treacle and lemon juice.

Serves 4

THE MEAT

8 lamb loin chops, about 175g (6oz) each, and
    3.5cm (1½in) thick
2 tbsp olive oil
1 tsp ground fennel seed
Kosher salt and freshly cracked black pepper to taste

THE RELISH

45g (1½oz) walnut halves
3 red peppers
2 tbsp extra virgin olive oil
4 tbsp roughly chopped fresh mint
2 tbsp pomegranate molasses
1 tsp finely chopped garlic
Kosher salt and freshly cracked black pepper to taste

Toast the walnuts: heat the oven to 180°C (350°F/Gas 4), spread the nuts over a shallow baking pan, and cook, checking frequently, until golden (5–10 minutes). Allow to cool, then roughly chop them.

Build a multilevel fire in your grill (*see p31*). When the coals are all ignited, the flames have died down, and the temperature is hot (*see p34*), you're ready to cook.

Put the red peppers on the hot side of the grill and cook, rolling them around, until the skins are completely black and blistered on all sides (8–12 minutes). Put them in a paper bag, fold it closed, and set aside until the peppers are cool enough to handle. Then gently pull the skin from the peppers, tear them open, remove the seeds, ribs, and stem, and dice them medium.

Rub the chops with the oil and sprinkle with the fennel, salt, and pepper. Place the chops on the hot side of the grill and sear well, about 6 minutes per side. Move the chops to the cooler side of the grill and cook, turning once, until done as you like (4–6 minutes more for rare). To check for doneness, make a cut in the thickest part of one chop and peek inside; it should be slightly less done than you like it. Remove the chops from the grill, cover them loosely with foil, and allow to rest for 5 minutes.

While the chops are cooking, combine all the relish ingredients in a medium bowl and mix well.

Put a generous spoonful of relish on each of four dishes, top with a chop, and pass the remaining relish on the side.

MEDITERRANEAN PORK CHOPS
WITH APRICOT-MINT RELISH

Spices from the Mediterranean make these pork chops taste at once familiar and slightly exotic; you could serve them twice a week without seeming too "out there" or boring your taste buds. An apricot relish brings freshness and a bit of heat to the party. This recipe makes more spice rub than you need, but it keeps well, and is great on lamb or chicken too.

Serves 4

THE MEAT

4 pork rib chops, 350–400g (12–14oz) each, about
   3.5cm (1½in) thick
2 tbsp olive oil

THE RELISH

3 ripe apricots, stoned and diced medium
4 tbsp roughly chopped fresh mint
Juice of ½ lemon (about 2 tbsp)
4 dashes of Tabasco sauce
Kosher salt and freshly cracked black pepper to taste

THE SPICE RUB

4 tbsp sesame seeds
5 tbsp coriander seeds, freshly cracked
2 tbsp ground fenugreek
2 tbsp dried oregano
1 tbsp ground cumin
1 tbsp kosher salt
Pinch of ground cinnamon

Build a multilevel fire in your grill (*see p31*). When the coals are all ignited, the flames have died down, and the temperature is medium (*see p34*), you're ready to cook.

For the spice rub, toast the sesame seeds in a dry frying pan on the grill, shaking them frequently to prevent burning, until they become just a shade darker (3–5 minutes).

Combine the spice rub ingredients in a small bowl and mix well. Measure out about 4 tbsp of the rub for the pork chops. Rub the chops with oil and coat them with the spice rub, pressing gently to be sure it adheres.

Put the chops on the grill over the hotter part of the fire and cook, turning once, until well-seared (3–4 minutes per side). Move the chops to the cooler side of the grill, cover them with a metal pie tin or disposable foil tray, and let them cook slowly until they are done to your liking (8–10 minutes per side for medium). To check for doneness, poke the chops with your finger to test their firmness (*see p37*); if you're unsure, make a small cut in the thickest part of one chop to be sure it is just slightly less done than you like it.

While the chops are on the grill, combine the apricots, mint, lemon juice, Tabasco, and salt and pepper in a small bowl and mix well. Transfer to a serving dish and set aside.

Transfer the chops to a serving plate and serve, passing the relish on the side.

GLAZED PORK MEDALLIONS WITH SMOKY SWEETCORN-RED PEPPER RELISH

If you make this dish with pork raised in the old-fashioned way so it has plenty of fat and flavour, it's going to be out of this world; but it is still fantastic even with today's leaner pork, because it has so many wonderful flavours going on in the glaze and the relish. If you have any relish left over, try it with simple grilled fish, or in any cold meat sandwich.

Serves 4

THE MEAT

5 tbsp treacle
30g (1oz) butter, melted
1 tbsp chilli pepper flakes
1 tbsp freshly cracked black pepper
8 boneless pork loin chops, 140g (5oz) each, about 2cm (¾in) thick
2 tbsp olive oil
Kosher salt and freshly cracked black pepper

THE RELISH

1 red pepper
3 ears sweetcorn, stripped of husks and silks
4 tbsp roughly chopped fresh basil
3 tbsp extra virgin olive oil
3 tbsp balsamic vinegar
1 tsp finely chopped fresh garlic
Kosher salt and freshly cracked black pepper to taste

Build a fire in your grill. When the coals are all ignited, the flames have died down, and the temperature is medium-hot (*see p34*), you're ready to cook.

For the relish, put the pepper on the grill, rolling it around until the skin is completely black and blistered on all sides (8–12 minutes). Put it in a paper bag, fold it closed, and set aside until the pepper is cool enough to handle. Then gently pull the skin from the pepper, tear it open, remove the seeds, ribs, and stem, and dice medium. While the pepper is cooling, put the ears of sweetcorn on the grill over the coals and cook, rolling them around occasionally, until they are starting to brown and are a little bit tender (3–4 minutes). Transfer the ears to a cutting board and slice the kernels off the cobs. Combine the roasted red pepper, toasted corn, basil, oil, vinegar, and garlic in a medium bowl and mix well. Season to taste with salt and pepper, then transfer the relish to a serving dish.

Make the glaze: combine the treacle, butter, chilli pepper flakes, and pepper in a small bowl and mix well.

Dry the pork chops with kitchen paper, rub them all over with the olive oil, and sprinkle them generously with salt and pepper. Put them on the grill directly over the coals and cook, turning once, until done to your liking (about 5 minutes per side for medium-well done). Brush them with the glaze during the last 30 seconds of cooking on each side. To check for doneness, poke the meat with your finger to test its firmness (*see p37*). If you're unsure, make a small cut in it; it should be just slightly less done than you like it. Transfer the chops to a serving plate, cover them loosely with foil, and let them rest for 5 minutes before serving with the relish and any remaining glaze.

COWBOY STEAK WITH BARBECUED LEEKS AND APRICOT MUSTARD

We love bone-in ribeye steaks – they are right up there on the tenderness scale, but because they are well-marbled they also have plenty of deep, beefy flavour. To accompany them, leeks make a nice change from the standard grilled onions, and in place of horseradish, we give you a super-quick way to perk up wholegrain mustard.

Serves 2

THE MEAT

1 tbsp ground cumin
1 tbsp ground coriander
1 tbsp chilli powder
2 tbsp kosher salt
30g (1oz) freshly cracked black pepper
900g (2lb) bone-in ribeye steak, about
    5cm (2in) thick
2 tbsp olive oil

THE LEEKS

4 leeks, white parts only, trimmed and very well washed
1 tbsp olive oil

THE MUSTARD

4 tbsp wholegrain mustard
2 tbsp finely chopped dried apricots

Build a multilevel fire in your grill (*see p31*). When the coals are all ignited, the flames have died down, and the temperature is hot (*see p34*), you're ready to cook.

Combine the cumin, coriander, chilli powder, salt, and pepper in a small bowl and mix well.

Rub the steak with some of the oil, then sprinkle it with about two-thirds of the spice mixture, pressing down gently to be sure it adheres. Put the steak on the grill directly over the hottest part of the fire and sear very well for 5–8 minutes per side, then move to the cooler part of the grill and continue to cook until it is done to your liking (8–10 minutes more per side for rare). To check for doneness, poke the meat with your finger to test its firmness (*see p37*). If you're unsure, make a cut into the centre; it should be just slightly less done than you like it. Remove from the grill, cover loosely with foil, and allow to rest for 5 minutes.

While the steak is searing, rub the leeks with the remaining oil and sprinkle with the remaining spice rub. When you move the steak to the cooler side of the grill, lay the leeks beside it and cook them, rolling around occasionally for even cooking, until they are golden-brown and slightly charred (8–12 minutes). Transfer the leeks to a cutting board, halve them lengthways, then slice crossways into half-moons about 1cm (½in) wide. Cover to keep warm until the steak is done.

Mix the mustard and the apricots together until evenly combined.

Transfer the steak to a serving plate (halved or sliced as you wish) and arrange the leeks, cut-side up, around the meat. Dab both with the apricot mustard and serve, passing additional mustard on the side.

GRILLED FILLET STEAK WITH GORGONZOLA, PANCETTA, AND PEACH-BALSAMIC JAM

Got a special occasion coming up? Looking for the most sumptuous steak dinner possible? Look no further. There's a reason that fillet steak is a byword for steak luxury – it's the single most tender cut of beef, with a meltingly smooth texture. In this Italian-influenced spin on the classic trio of steak, blue cheese, and bacon, we top the steak with a little slab of Gorgonzola cheese and scatter pancetta over the top. For the final touch, we add a fresh peach jam with Italian flavours. Now, that's a celebration.

Serves 4

THE STEAKS

225g (8oz) pancetta, diced small (or substitute bacon)

4 beef fillet steaks, 225–280g (8–10oz) each, about 5cm (2in) thick

2 tbsp olive oil

Kosher salt and freshly cracked black pepper to taste

225g (8oz) Gorgonzola cheese, cut into 4 pieces

THE JAM

2 tbsp olive oil

1 medium red onion, peeled and diced small

3 ripe but firm peaches, stoned and diced medium

5 tbsp balsamic vinegar

5 tbsp freshly squeezed orange juice

1 tbsp soft dark brown sugar

Kosher salt and freshly cracked black pepper to taste

Make the jam: on the hob, heat the olive oil in a large sauté pan over a medium-high heat until hot but not smoking. Add the onion and cook, stirring occasionally, until translucent (7–9 minutes). Add the peaches and cook, stirring frequently, for another 3 minutes – you just want the peaches to be nicely softened. Add the vinegar, orange juice, brown sugar, and salt and pepper and bring to the boil. Reduce the heat to medium-low and simmer until the jam begins to thicken (8–10 minutes). Remove from the heat and set aside.

Build a multilevel fire in your grill (*see p31*). When the coals are all ignited, the flames have died down, and the temperature is hot (*see p34*), you're ready to cook.

While the fire heats up, sauté the pancetta on the hob over a medium-low heat, turning frequently until it is crisp and brown – about 7 minutes. Transfer to kitchen paper to drain, then to a small bowl; cover to keep warm.

Rub the steaks with oil and sprinkle generously with salt and pepper. When the grill is ready, put the steaks over the hottest coals and sear well for 6–8 minutes per side. Move the steaks to the cooler part of the fire, cover with a pie tin or disposable foil tray, and cook for another 8–10 minutes, until done to your liking. To check for doneness, poke the meat with your finger to test its firmness (*see p37*); if you're unsure, cut into it and look to be sure it is just slightly less done than you like it.

Transfer the steaks to a serving plate and top with the cheese. Cover loosely with foil and allow the steaks to rest and the cheese to melt for about 5 minutes. Sprinkle over the pancetta and serve with the jam on the side.

GLAZED PORK TENDERLOIN
WITH DATE-SAGE RELISH

Pork tenderloin, a lovely little roast, is ideal for the grill because it cooks in just a few minutes and is congenial to a whole range of flavours. Here we coat it with spicy mustard seeds before it goes over the coals, then brush it with a pungent-sweet mix of honey and mustard just before it comes off the grill (so the honey doesn't burn). To round out the flavour palette, we serve the meat with an earthy and sweet date-sage relish.

Serves 4

THE MEAT

2 pork tenderloins, 350–400g (12–14oz) each
Kosher salt
3 tbsp brown mustard seeds
3 tbsp freshly cracked black pepper
3 tbsp olive oil
4 tbsp wholegrain mustard
4 tbsp honey

THE RELISH

1 tbsp freshly cracked coriander seeds (or substitute 1½ tsp ground coriander)
4 tbsp stoned, diced dates
Juice of ½ orange (about 4 tbsp)
Juice of I lemon (about 4 tbsp)
4 tbsp roughly chopped fresh parsley
2 tbsp roughly chopped fresh sage
1 tbsp peeled and finely chopped fresh ginger
1 tbsp finely chopped orange zest

Build a fire in your grill. When the coals are all ignited, the fire has died down, and the temperature is medium (*see p34*), you're ready to cook.

Toast the coriander seeds for the relish, if using, in a dry frying pan on the grill, shaking them frequently to avoid burning, until they become fragrant and are just a shade darker (3–5 minutes).

Dry the tenderloins well with kitchen paper and sprinkle generously with salt. Combine the mustard seeds, black pepper, and oil in a small bowl and mix well. Rub this mixture all over the meat, pressing gently to make it adhere.

Whisk the mustard and honey together in another small bowl until well-blended.

Put the tenderloins on the grill over the coals and cook, rolling them around every 3–4 minutes for even cooking, until they are done to your liking (12–15 minutes for medium). Brush the tenderloins all over with the honey mustard during the last 30 seconds of cooking. To check for doneness, poke the meat with your finger to check its firmness (*see p37*). If you're unsure, make a cut in the thickest part of one of the tenderloins; it should be slightly less done than you like it. Transfer the tenderloins to a cutting board and cover them loosely with foil to keep warm.

While the tenderloins are resting, combine all the relish ingredients in a small bowl and toss gently.

Carve the pork into 1cm (½in) thick slices, and arrange these on a serving plate. Drizzle with the honey mustard, and pass the relish on the side.

HARISSA-RUBBED GRILLED SKIRT STEAK WITH ORANGE-FENNEL RELISH

This dish is for true heat fanatics. Although lamb would be more typically Moroccan, we think the fiery complexity of harissa and the bright, cooling flavours of this relish work perfectly with rich, meaty skirt steak too. If you're in a hurry or are not particularly fussy, you can just chop the oranges into chunks rather than peeling off all the membrane.

Serves 4

THE MEAT

1kg (2½lb) trimmed skirt steak, cut into 4 pieces
Kosher salt and freshly cracked black pepper

THE RELISH

1 fennel bulb, trimmed, cored, and finely sliced
1 large orange
2 tbsp red wine vinegar
2 tbsp roughly chopped fresh mint
Kosher salt and freshly cracked black pepper to taste

THE HARISSA

4 tbsp olive oil
4 tbsp chilli pepper flakes (or crushed dried red chillies of your choice)
2 tbsp freshly cracked coriander seeds, toasted (see opposite), or substitute 1 tbsp ground coriander
2 tbsp cumin seeds
1 tbsp fennel seeds
1 tbsp finely chopped fresh garlic

Build a multilevel fire in your grill (*see p31*). When the coals are all ignited, the fire has died down, and the temperature is medium (*see p34*), you're ready to cook.

Make the relish: on the hob, bring a pan of salted water to the boil. Add the fennel and cook for 2 minutes. Drain well, and allow it to cool. Peel the orange with a sharp knife, removing all the white pith. Working over a bowl to catch the juice, cut between the membranes and remove each orange segment whole, discarding the pips. Put the orange segments in another bowl. Measure 2 tbsp of the juice, and add it to the orange segments, along with the blanched fennel, vinegar, mint, and salt and pepper. Mix well and set aside.

Make the harissa: mash the oil, chilli, coriander, cumin, fennel, and garlic into a paste. Dry the steaks well with kitchen paper, season them generously with salt and pepper, then rub the paste on both sides.

When the fire is ready, put the steaks on the grill over the hottest coals and sear them well on one side (about 4 minutes). Turn the steaks and continue to cook until done to your liking (4–5 minutes more for medium-rare). To check for doneness, poke each steak with your finger to test its firmness (*see p37*). If you're unsure, make a cut in the thickest part of one steak; it should be slightly less done than you like. Transfer the steaks to a cutting board, cover loosely with foil, and allow them to rest for 5 minutes.

Thinly slice the steaks diagonally across the grain and serve, with the relish on the side.

ORIENTAL PORK RIBS

The first time I (Chris) ever had ribs was in a Chinese restaurant in the Virginia town where I grew up. Even now, when I think of ribs the first thing that pops up in my flavour memory is the taste of those "pupu platter" favourites. But this updated version has deeper, more powerful flavours; plus, with its grill-and-toss approach, it's easier to make. If you're serving these as finger food at a party – for which they are perfect – you should make twice as many as you think you need, because they're going to disappear fast.

Serves 6 as an appetizer

THE MEAT

2 racks baby back ribs, about 900g (2lb) each
2 tbsp vegetable oil
Kosher salt and freshly cracked white pepper
    (or substitute black) to taste

THE SAUCE

5 tbsp finely crushed roasted peanuts
4 tbsp roughly chopped spring onions, green
    and white parts
4 tbsp hoisin sauce
4 tbsp soy sauce
4 tbsp rice wine vinegar
3 tbsp sesame oil
2 tbsp sriracha (Southeast Asian hot chilli-garlic
    sauce, available in Asian markets or large
    supermarkets)
2 tbsp peeled and finely chopped fresh ginger

Light a fire well over to one side of your grill, using enough coals to fill half a shoebox.

Rub the ribs with oil and sprinkle them generously with salt and pepper.

When the fire has died down and the coals are covered in white ash, place the ribs on the side of the grill away from the coals, being careful that none of the meat is directly over the coals. Put the lid on the grill with the vents open one-quarter of the way and cook for 20 minutes. Flip the ribs and cook them for an additional 20 minutes.

Meanwhile, combine the ingredients for the sauce in a very large bowl and mix well.

When the ribs are done, transfer them to a cutting board. Cut the racks apart, adding the ribs to the bowl of sauce as they are separated. Toss the ribs with the sauce until thoroughly coated, and serve immediately – with lots of paper napkins.

WATER-DWELLERS

TAKE A LOOK AT THE BEACHES OF THE TROPICAL WORLD AND YOU'LL UNDERSTAND THE LONG-STANDING (AND VERY DELICIOUS) RELATIONSHIP BETWEEN SEAFOOD AND LIVE-FIRE COOKING. AND SINCE WE LOVE BEACHES AND THE TROPICS, WE ARE HUGE FANS OF FISH AND OTHER SEA CREATURES ON THE GRILL. WITH THESE RECIPES, WE THINK YOU WILL BE, TOO.

GRILL-SEARED DOUBLE-THICK TUNA STEAKS WITH PICKLED GINGER, WASABI, AND SOY

Twenty-two years ago, on the day that I (Chris) opened the doors of my restaurant, the East Coast Grill, in Cambridge, Massachusetts, this dish was on the menu. All these years later, it is still the most popular single item we serve. The key to this dish lies in its simplicity; the sole determining factor of success or failure is getting absolutely super-fresh, sushi-quality tuna. Make sure that you cut it really thick and cook it the way you like your steak. We think it tastes best rare but, as with all food, it's your choice. Pickled ginger and wasabi should be available at a good Asian food store or larger supermarket. Alternatively, you can order from speciality Japanese food retailers online.

Serves 4

THE INGREDIENTS

4 tbsp sesame seeds
4 super-fresh tuna steaks, 225–280g (8–10oz) each,
 about 7.5cm (3in) thick
3 tbsp sesame oil
2 tbsp freshly cracked white pepper
2 tbsp kosher salt
4 spring onions, ends trimmed, cut into thin strips
4 tbsp pickled ginger
3 tbsp wasabi powder, mixed with water to the
 consistency of wet sand
5 tbsp dark soy sauce, preferably aged

Build a fire in your grill. When the coals are all ignited, the flames have died down, and the temperature is hot (*see p34*), you're ready to cook.

Lightly toast the sesame seeds in a dry frying pan on the grill, shaking them frequently to prevent burning, until they are just a shade darker. (You can alternatively do this over a medium heat on the hob.) Set them aside.

Rub the tuna steaks all over with the sesame oil, sprinkle with the white pepper and salt, then put them on the grill directly over the coals and sear well on both sides (4–5 minutes per side). When you have a dark brown, crispy crust on both sides, grill the steaks on each of the 4 edges for about 2 minutes, aiming to achieve the same dark, crusty effect. Transfer to a serving plate or individual plates.

Scatter the spring onions and sesame seeds over the tuna, and serve with the pickled ginger, wasabi, and soy sauce on the side.

BRICK-GRILLED SQUID WITH LEMON, CHILLI, CORIANDER, AND GARLIC

Here we take a technique that is typically used with chicken – holding it flat against the grill with a brick, so that it gets a really nice overall sear from the flames – and apply it to squid. This has the added advantage of making sure that the squid cooks really quickly, which keeps it from toughening up. Plus, it's always fun to have guests wondering why you need a foil-wrapped brick to make dinner.

Serves 4 as an appetizer

THE SQUID

675g (1½lb) cleaned squid with tentacles (separate these from the squid bodies, or ask your fishmonger to do so), thoroughly rinsed and drained well

2 tbsp olive oil
1 tbsp chilli pepper flakes
Kosher salt and freshly cracked black pepper to taste

THE DRESSING

5 tbsp roughly chopped fresh coriander
4 tbsp extra virgin olive oil
Juice of 1 lemon (about 4 tbsp)
1 tsp finely chopped garlic
7 dashes of Tabasco sauce, or to taste

Build a fire in your grill. When the coals are all ignited, the fire has died down, and the temperature is hot (*see p34*), you're ready to cook. Wrap a clean brick with foil and place it by your grill.

Put the squid in a large bowl, add the olive oil, chilli flakes, and salt and pepper, and toss gently to coat. Thread the tentacles onto skewers so they don't fall through the grill when you cook them.

Combine the coriander, olive oil, lemon juice, garlic, and Tabasco in a large bowl. Mix well and set aside.

Arrange a few squid bodies on the grill over the coals, and cover them completely with the brick. Cook until opaque throughout, about 2 minutes per side, then remove the brick and allow the bodies to cook for about 30 seconds longer, until they are golden brown and crisp. Repeat this process with the rest of the squid bodies, adding the tentacles to the grill (no brick required) with the last batch. Cook the tentacles for about 2 minutes, until they are evenly brown and crisp.

Slice the squid bodies into rings and add them, along with the tentacles, to the lemon-garlic dressing, tossing to coat. Pile the squid onto a serving plate and serve.

PORTUGAL: THE FISH THAT CHANGED IT ALL

When people ask, as they sometimes do, what is the best meal I (Doc) have ever eaten, one of the top contenders is a very simple lunch I had years ago on the beach in southern Portugal.

I was travelling with friends and, since we were on a very strict budget, we decided to camp out on the beach instead of staying in a hotel. Fortunately, not far from our makeshift campsite was a small, open-air restaurant, really nothing more than a handful of tables with a roof over them, right on the sand. There wasn't much in the way of equipment – a wood-burning grill, a hot plate, and a large cooler – and when we arrived there didn't seem to be much food, either. It looked like some greens and maybe some fried potatoes were about all we could look forward to. But there was cold white wine in the cooler, and it was a beautiful day, so we settled in. Unfortunately, we couldn't seem to get our hosts to serve us any food. After about half an hour, though, we discovered why: the main course was just arriving. A small fishing boat pulled up right on the beach and several men jumped out and brought pails of fish up the dunes. The young cook paid for them, quickly cleaned them, and threw them on the wood fire that he had built up when the boat came into sight. I must admit, though, that I was a little apprehensive. These fish, I was told by my friends, were sardines, and I had never been a fan of dark-fleshed, oily fish. But this meal changed that forever. The salad was crisp and refreshing, the potatoes earthy and satisfying, but the sardines stole the show. Hot off the grill, with crispy skin and rich, dark, succulent flesh, they were a revelation. Oily fish became my friends, and still are to this day.

GRILLED SARDINES
WITH LEMON AND PAPRIKA

Fresh sardines are wonderful fish for the grill, with a delicious, meaty taste. Here we simply top them with some traditional Portuguese flavours, then grill them up. For a slightly more exotic approach, try replacing the ordinary paprika with *pimentón de La Vera*, a Spanish smoked paprika with a distinctive smoky flavour.

Serves 4 as an appetizer

4 tbsp extra virgin olive oil
1 tsp minced garlic
1 tsp good-quality paprika
12 fresh sardines
2 lemons, one halved and one cut into quarters
4 tbsp roughly chopped fresh parsley
Kosher salt and freshly cracked black pepper

Build a fire in your grill. When the coals are all ignited, the flames have died down, and the temperature is hot (*see p34*), you're ready to cook.

Mix together the olive oil, garlic, and paprika in a small bowl. Pour this mixture over the sardines, then squeeze the two lemon halves over them and sprinkle with the parsley and salt and pepper to taste.

Put the sardines on the grill directly over the coals and cook until they are nicely seared on the outside and just opaque on the inside (3–4 minutes per side). To check for doneness, manipulate one of the sardines so you can see inside it at its thickest point to be sure it is just opaque all the way through.

Serve with lemon quarters for squeezing.

CUMIN SALMON FILLETS
WITH CHILLI-ORANGE BUTTER

Salmon works perfectly on the grill, because it has a firm enough texture not to fall apart, and its strong, rich, defined taste can stand up to the grill flavour. Here we challenge the salmon further with a quick cumin rub and a flavoured butter featuring hot, smoky chipotle pepper along with a combination of other Latin ingredients. Fortunately, the fish is up to the challenge, and the resulting dish is spectacular.

Serves 4

THE FISH

3 tbsp freshly cracked cumin seeds
  (or substitute 1½ tbsp ground cumin)
4 salmon fillets, about 225g (8oz) each (or substitute halibut)
2 tbsp olive oil
Kosher salt and freshly cracked black pepper to taste

THE BUTTER

2 tbsp finely chopped chipotle peppers in adobo sauce
2 tbsp roughly chopped fresh coriander
Juice of 1 lime (about 2 tbsp)
1 tbsp finely chopped orange zest
60g (2oz) unsalted butter, softened
Kosher salt and freshly cracked black pepper

Make the butter: combine the chipotles, coriander, lime juice, orange zest, and butter in a small bowl and mash together until evenly blended. Add salt and pepper to taste. Wrap the butter in cling film, shape it into a log, and refrigerate until firm. (This butter will keep in the refrigerator for a week, or frozen for several months.)

Toast the cumin seeds (if using) on the stove top in a dry frying pan over a medium heat, shaking them frequently to prevent burning, until they are fragrant and just a shade darker (3–5 minutes). Set them aside.

Build a fire in your grill. When the coals are all ignited, the flames have died down, and the temperature is medium (*see p34*), you're ready to cook.

Rub the salmon fillets on both sides with olive oil, sprinkle generously with salt and pepper, then rub the cumin into the salmon, pressing gently so it adheres. Put the fillets on the grill over the coals and cook until almost opaque throughout (6–8 minutes per side). To check for doneness, poke the fish with your finger to test its firmness (*see p37*). If you're unsure, make a cut in the thickest part of the fillet to be sure it is nearly opaque all the way through. Transfer the salmon to a serving plate, and top each hot fillet with a slice or two of the seasoned butter.

GRILLED SWORDFISH STEAKS WITH SMOKED SALMON-CHIVE BUTTER

If you're apprehensive about grilling fish, this recipe is a great one for sharpening your skills. The solid, meaty texture of swordfish makes it ideal for the grill – it's really no more difficult than a steak – and its mild-tasting white flesh is ideal for pairing with a range of distinct flavours. Plus, if you make the salmon-chive butter in advance (it keeps in the refrigerator for several days, and in the freezer for a couple of months), you can come home from work and have this dish on the table in no time at all.

Serves 4

THE FISH

4 swordfish steaks, 225g (8oz) each, about 2.5cm (1in) thick
2 tbsp olive oil
3 tbsp freshly cracked black pepper
1 tbsp kosher salt

THE BUTTER

115g (4oz) unsalted butter, softened
60g (2oz) smoked salmon, roughly chopped
Juice of ½ a lemon (about 2 tbsp)
5 dashes of Tabasco sauce
3 tbsp finely chopped fresh chives
Kosher salt and freshly cracked black pepper to taste

Build a fire in your grill. When the coals are all ignited, the flames have died down, and the temperature is hot (*see p34*), you're ready to cook.

Rub the fish steaks with the oil and coat them generously with the pepper and salt, pressing gently so it adheres. Put the steaks on the grill directly over the coals and cook until they are just opaque throughout (5–7 minutes per side). To check for doneness, poke the fish with your finger to test its firmness (*see p37*); if you're unsure, make a cut in one of the steaks to be sure it is just opaque all the way through.

While the swordfish is on the grill, combine the butter, salmon, lemon juice, and Tabasco in a food processor and blend until smooth. Add the chives and salt and pepper to taste and pulse a few times to blend.

When the fish is done, arrange the steaks on a serving plate, top each one with some of the salmon-chive butter, and serve immediately.

GRILLED BASS WITH MEDITERRANEAN SALAD

We are lucky enough to spend a lot of time on the southern coast of Massachusetts, and (when we're even luckier) we sometimes catch striped bass there. This simple summer dish is one of our favourite ways to prepare it – the subtly-flavoured, big-flaked fish is perfect grilled very plainly (*see overleaf*), then nicely complemented by the restrained flavours of the tomato cucumber salad. If you can't find striped bass, sea bass is just as delicious prepared this way.

Serves 4

THE FISH

4 sea bass or striped bass fillets, 225g (8oz) each
2 tablespoons vegetable oil
Kosher salt and freshly cracked black pepper

THE SALAD

2 tomatoes about the size of tennis balls, cored and
    diced large
1 cucumber, peeled if desired, diced medium
½ red onion, peeled and diced small
60g (2oz) pitted black olives

THE DRESSING

Juice of 1½ lemons (about 5 tbsp)
4 tbsp finely chopped fresh basil
Pinch of chilli pepper flakes
Kosher salt and freshly cracked black pepper to taste
5 tbsp extra virgin olive oil

Build a multilevel fire (*see p31*) in your grill. When the coals are all ignited, the flames have died down, and the temperature is medium (*see p34*), you're ready to cook.

Rub the bass fillets with the vegetable oil and sprinkle them generously with salt and pepper. Place the fillets on the hotter side of the grill and cook until they develop a crusty, dark sear on the outside and are opaque on the inside (6–8 minutes per side). If the flesh starts to become too dark, move the fillets to the cooler side of the grill and cover them with a pie tin or disposable foil tray to finish cooking. To check for doneness, poke the fish with your finger to test its firmness (*see p37*); if you're unsure, make a cut in one of the fillets to be sure it is just opaque all the way through.

While the fish is cooking, put the salad ingredients in a medium bowl. Combine all the dressing ingredients except the olive oil in a small bowl, then add the oil, whisking, and whisk until well-blended. Add just enough of this dressing to moisten the salad mixture and toss until well-blended and evenly coated with dressing.

To serve, divide the salad among four dinner plates and arrange a grilled fillet over each.

OYSTERS WITH PANCETTA

Some people eat only raw oysters; others eat only cooked ones. We happen to be members of both clubs. This dish is in the great grilled oyster tradition that's found in the bays and inlets of the Pacific coast north of San Francisco, where you can go buy a bag of oysters and a bag of charcoal and cook 'em yourself right on the scene. There's not much that's better than that. Here we accompany the oysters with a simple barbecue sauce and, in keeping with our belief that almost anything goes better with a little cured pork, top them with some pancetta.

Serves 4 as an appetizer

THE INGREDIENTS

225g (8 oz) pancetta, diced small
45g (1½oz) butter
4 tbsp tomato ketchup
Juice of 1 lemon (about 4 tbsp)
2 tbsp roughly chopped fresh parsley
6 dashes of Tabasco sauce
3 dashes of Worcestershire sauce
Kosher salt and freshly cracked black pepper to taste
24 oysters of your choice, shells scrubbed

Build a fire in your grill. When the coals are all ignited, the fire has died down, and the temperature is medium (*see p34*), you're ready to cook.

While you wait for the fire, cook the pancetta on the hob in a large sauté pan over a medium-low heat, stirring frequently until it is crisp and brown (about 7 minutes). Transfer to kitchen paper to drain.

Melt the butter in a small saucepan. Whisk in the ketchup, lemon juice, half of the parsley (reserve the rest for garnishing), Tabasco, Worcestershire sauce, and salt and pepper, and remove from the heat.

Shuck the oysters and loosen them in their bottom shells. Arrange the oysters (in their bottom shells) on the grill over the coals, and cook just until their edges start to ruffle (2–3 minutes). Spoon about 1 tbsp sauce over each oyster, and continue to cook until the sauce is bubbling hot. Transfer to a serving plate, sprinkle with parsley and pancetta, and serve, but be careful – the oyster shells will be very hot.

CAJUN GROUPER WITH TABASCO-SWEETCORN TARTAR SAUCE

Back in the 1980s, Cajun cooking suddenly became very popular in the US, and everyone wanted blackened redfish. This is our version of that approach, in which fish is coated with a spice rub and put over the fire to blacken the mixture, which gives the fish a nice crust. (If you can't find grouper, you can substitute sea bass, or red snapper.) And the spicy tartar sauce, with the nice crunch of sweetcorn kernels and the sweetness of gherkins, goes with just about any white-fleshed fish, however it's prepared.

Serves 4

THE FISH

3 tbsp paprika
2 tbsp ground coriander
2 tbsp kosher salt
1 tbsp mustard powder
1 tbsp ground black pepper
1 tbsp cayenne pepper
4 grouper steaks or fillets, 225–280g (8–10oz) each
3 tbsp olive oil

THE SAUCE

1 ear sweetcorn, stripped of husks and silks
140g (5oz) prepared mayonnaise
4 tbsp finely chopped gherkins
3 tbsp roughly chopped fresh parsley
2–3 tbsp Tabasco (or other hot sauce of your choice), or use as much or little as you prefer
2 tbsp made brown mustard
1 tbsp celery seeds
Kosher salt and freshly cracked black pepper to taste

For the sauce: on the hob, bring a large pan of salted water to the boil and blanch the ear of sweetcorn for 2 minutes. Drain and cut the kernels off the cob.

Combine the sweetcorn kernels with the rest of the sauce ingredients in a small bowl and mix well. Transfer to a serving bowl, cover, and refrigerate until serving time.

Build a fire in your grill. When the coals are all ignited, the flames have died down, and the temperature is medium (*see p34*), you're ready to cook.

Combine the paprika, coriander, kosher salt, mustard powder, black pepper, and cayenne pepper in a small bowl and mix well. Rub the grouper with olive oil and coat it generously on all sides with the spice mixture, pressing gently to be sure it adheres. Put the fish on the grill directly over the coals and cook until it is just opaque throughout (6–8 minutes per side). To check for doneness, poke the fish with your finger to test its firmness (*see p37*); if you're unsure, make a cut in one of the steaks or fillets to be sure it is opaque all the way through.

Transfer the fish to a serving plate and serve, passing the tartar sauce on the side.

MONKFISH WITH SPICY VINAIGRETTE

The dense, meaty texture and mild, sweetish flavour of monkfish have made it a favourite of grillers. Although it is often called "poor man's lobster", it is actually more able to stand up to strong flavours than lobster is. In this simple dish we take advantage of that trait by coating the fish with cumin and coriander before it goes over the coals, then drizzling it with a spicy vinaigrette that features flavours of Latin America.

Serves 4

THE FISH

3 tbsp freshly cracked cumin seeds
2 tbsp ground coriander
Kosher salt and freshly cracked black pepper to taste
4 monkfish fillets, about 225g (8oz) each
2 tbsp olive oil

THE VINAIGRETTE

5 tbsp extra virgin olive oil
Juice of 2 limes (about 4 tbsp)
3 tbsp roughly chopped fresh oregano
1 tbsp finely chopped fresh chilli pepper of your choice, or to taste
1 tsp finely chopped fresh garlic
Kosher salt and freshly cracked black pepper to taste

Build a fire in your grill. When the coals are all ignited, the flames have died down, and the temperature is medium-hot (*see p34*), you're ready to cook.

Combine the cumin, coriander, and salt and pepper in a small bowl and mix well. Rub the fillets with the oil and coat them generously with this mixture, pressing gently so it adheres. Put on the grill and cook until just opaque throughout (6–8 minutes per side). To check for doneness, poke the fish with your finger to test its firmness (*see p37*); if you're unsure, make a cut in one of the fillets to be sure it is just opaque all the way through.

While the fish is on the grill, combine the vinaigrette ingredients in a small bowl and whisk until well-blended.

Transfer the fillets to a serving plate, drizzle generously with vinaigrette, and serve, passing the remaining vinaigrette on the side.

FLAVOUR FOOTPRINT SOUTHEAST ASIA

Over the past couple of decades, the cuisines of Southeast Asia have truly come into their own on the international culinary stage. Perhaps their most salient characteristic is a tendency to combine hot, sour, sweet, and salty all in the same dish, so that each mouthful is a kaleidoscope of flavours. Often this riot of tastes is deepened and united by the judicious use of fermented seafood products, of which fish sauce (stocked by most large supermarkets) is perhaps the most amenable to Western taste buds; if you want to experiment with others, check out your local Southeast Asian grocery. We love the explosive nature of Southeast Asian flavours, and after you try out a couple of these easy seasonings we think you will, too.

Southeast Asian-Style Spice Paste
Makes about 140g (5oz)

Brush or rub this fiery curry paste all over any cut of lamb or beef before grilling.

2 tbsp sesame oil

3 tbsp vegetable oil

2 tbsp crushed coriander seeds

4 tbsp finely chopped jalapeño or other fresh chilli pepper of your choice

2 tbsp peeled and finely chopped fresh ginger

2 stalks lemongrass, finely chopped (use the tender inner portion of the bottom third of the stalk only)

2 tbsp finely chopped fresh garlic

1 tbsp ground white pepper

2 tsp kosher salt

Combine all the ingredients in a small bowl and mix well or, if you prefer a finer paste, crush together in a pestle and mortar, still leaving it somewhat chunky. This paste will keep, covered and refrigerated, for 2–3 days.

Southeast Asian Spice Rub
Makes about 115g (4oz)

Rub this dry spice mixture on any large piece of meat or fowl that you're going to grill.

4 tbsp curry powder

4 tbsp ground coriander

2 tbsp ground cumin

2 tbsp ground white pepper

2 tbsp kosher salt

1 tbsp turmeric

1 tbsp ground ginger

1 tbsp cayenne pepper

Combine all the ingredients in a small bowl and mix well. Stored in an airtight container in a cool, dark place, this rub will keep for months.

Southeast Asian-Style Spice Paste

Chilli-Fish Dipping Sauce
Makes about 240ml (8fl oz)

A simple but versatile dipping sauce to accompany skewers of chicken, fish, shrimp, or pork.

5 tbsp Thai fish sauce
Juice of 3 limes (about 6 tbsp)
2 jalapeño or other fresh chilli peppers of your choice, sliced into thin rounds
2 tsp granulated sugar

Combine all the ingredients in a small bowl and mix until the sugar dissolves. This sauce will keep, covered and refrigerated, for 4–5 days.

Mango-Ginger Relish
Makes about 340g (12oz)

This relish is a great accompaniment to just about anything grilled, but we particularly like it with seafood or chicken.

1 large, ripe but firm mango, peeled, stoned, and diced small
4 tbsp roughly chopped spring onions, including green tops
Juice of 2 limes (about 4 tbsp)
2 tbsp peeled and finely chopped fresh ginger
2 tbsp Thai fish sauce
1 tbsp finely chopped fresh chilli pepper of your choice

Combine all the ingredients in a medium bowl and mix well. This relish will keep, covered and refrigerated, for 2–3 days.

Peach-Chilli Sambal
Makes about 280g (10oz)

The chilli-fired seasonings called sambals originated in Malaysia and Indonesia, but are now found all over Southeast Asia as well as southern Africa. This peach-based version is great with pork, lamb, or full-flavoured fish like mackerel or bluefish.

2 ripe but firm peaches, peeled, stoned, and diced small
2 tbsp finely chopped jalapeño or other fresh chilli pepper of your choice
2 tbsp roughly chopped fresh coriander
2 tbsp Thai fish sauce
1 tbsp peeled and finely chopped fresh ginger
Juice of 1½ limes (about 3 tbsp)
1 tsp granulated sugar

Combine all the ingredients in a medium bowl and mix well. Serve this one right away; the peaches won't hold up too long.

Mango-Ginger Relish

SIGNATURE INGREDIENTS/TOP ROW (LEFT TO RIGHT) Fresh coriander, coriander seeds, fish sauce, lemongrass; **SECOND ROW** Lime leaves, garlic, red shallots, Thai basil; **THIRD ROW** Fresh mint, dried shrimp, ginger, tamarind; **BOTTOM ROW** Fresh chillies, coconut milk, shrimp paste, galangal.

HALIBUT WITH LIME-CHILLI MAYO AND SPICY PECANS

Mayonnaise and fish might seem like an odd combo, but once you taste this version, we think you'll understand why it's a classic. If you like, you can prepare both the mayonnaise mixture and the pecans in advance. Keep the mayo refrigerated and the pecans at room temperature, then all you'll have to do when your guests arrive is grill the halibut and you're ready to go. (The spicy pecans make a great snack on their own, by the way.)

Serves 4

THE FISH

4 halibut steaks, about 225g (8oz) each
2 tbsp olive oil
Kosher salt and freshly cracked black pepper

THE MAYO

225g (8oz) prepared mayonnaise
Juice of 1 lime (about 2 tbsp)
2 tbsp roughly chopped fresh coriander
1 chipotle pepper in adobo sauce, finely chopped

THE PECANS

45g (1½oz) pecans, lightly crushed
1 tsp olive oil
Pinch of granulated sugar
Pinch of chilli powder
Pinch of ground cumin
Pinch of cayenne pepper
Kosher salt and freshly cracked black pepper to taste

Build a fire in your grill. When the coals are all ignited, the flames have died down, and the temperature is medium-hot (*see p34*), you're ready to cook.

In the meantime, combine the mayonnaise, lime juice, coriander, and chipotle in a small bowl and mix well.

Combine the pecans, oil, sugar, and spices in a small sauté pan or frying pan and toast on the hob over a medium heat, stirring frequently, just until fragrant (about 5 minutes). Transfer to a small bowl to cool.

Rub the halibut with oil and sprinkle it generously with salt and pepper, then put it on the grill directly over the coals and cook until it is just opaque throughout (5–6 minutes per side). To check for doneness, poke the fish with your finger to test its firmness (*see p37*); if you're unsure, make a cut in one of the steaks at its thickest point to be sure it is just opaque all the way through.

Arrange the halibut steaks on a serving plate, drizzle generously with mayo, and scatter the pecans over the top.

GRILLED MAHI-MAHI
WITH AVOCADO-SWEETCORN SALSA

This subtropical fish ranges so widely in the ocean that is has several names – we call it by its Hawaiian name, which means "strong-strong", but it's also known as "dorado" and as "dolphin fish" because it often swims with dolphins. It is perhaps the most beautiful of game fish; when just out of the water, it displays a range of electric blues and greens and bright golds and silvers. It's also wonderful on the grill – mild-tasting, with a large, tender flake.

Serves 4 as an appetizer

THE FISH

- 1 tbsp each: chilli powder, ground cumin, and ground coriander
- 4 mahi-mahi fillets, about 225g (8oz) each (or substitute swordfish, halibut, or shark fillet)
- 2 tbsp olive oil
- Kosher salt and freshly cracked black pepper

THE SALSA

- 2 ears sweetcorn, stripped of husks and silks
- 1 ripe but firm avocado, stoned, peeled, and diced small
- Juice of 3 limes (about 5 tbsp)
- 4 tbsp roughly chopped fresh coriander
- 3 tbsp olive oil
- 1 tsp finely chopped jalapeño or other fresh chilli pepper of your choice
- Kosher salt and freshly cracked black pepper to taste

Blanch the sweetcorn for the salsa: on the hob, bring a large pan of salted water to the boil. Cook the ears for 2 minutes, drain, and cut the kernels off the cobs.

Combine the salsa ingredients in a medium bowl and mix gently but thoroughly. Cover with cling film and refrigerate until serving time.

Build a fire in your grill. When the coals are all ignited, the flames have died down, and the temperature is medium-hot (*see p34*), you're ready to cook.

Combine the chilli powder, cumin, and coriander in a small bowl and mix well. Rub the fish fillets on both sides with oil, sprinkle generously with salt and pepper, and rub all over with the spice mixture. Put the fillets over the coals and cook until just opaque all the way through (5–6 minutes per side). To check for doneness, poke the fish with your finger to test its firmness level (*see p37*); if you're unsure, make a cut in one of the fillets at its thickest point to be sure it is just opaque all the way through.

When the fish is done, put a fish fillet on each plate, top with a spoonful of the salsa, and pass the remaining salsa on the side.

PEEL 'N' EAT PRAWNS WITH OLD BAY SEASONING, BASIL, AND LEMON

Here's a celebration of the intimacy and informality of eating with your fingers. I (Chris) grew up in the mid-Atlantic states of the USA, and as a youth attended many a "shrimp boil", where the flavouring trick was to dump the distinctive spice mixture called Old Bay Seasoning into the water that the seafood was cooked in. Here we ring a little change on that tradition by grilling the shrimp first, then tossing them with a flavourful mixture featuring Old Bay. Try this one with a super-cold lager.

Serves 4 as an appetizer

THE INGREDIENTS

450g (1lb) raw prawns, 16/20 size, shell-on
2 tbsp olive oil
Kosher salt and freshly cracked black pepper to taste
Juice of 2 lemons (about 120ml/4fl oz)
4 tbsp roughly chopped fresh basil
45g (1½oz) butter, at room temperature
2 tbsp finely chopped garlic
1 tbsp Old Bay Seasoning (can be purchased on the internet)
6 dashes of Tabasco sauce
Kosher salt and freshly cracked black pepper to taste

Build a fire in your grill. When the coals are all ignited, the fire has died down, and the temperature is medium (*see p34*), you're ready to cook.

Using a small, sharp knife or small scissors, slit the shell along the back of each prawn, and remove the vein.

Toss the prawns with the oil and salt and pepper in a large bowl. Put the prawns on the grill over the coals and cook until they are opaque throughout (4–5 minutes per side). To check for doneness, cut into one of the prawns at its thickest point to be sure it is opaque all the way through.

While the prawns are cooking, combine the lemon juice, basil, butter, garlic, Old Bay Seasoning, Tabasco, and salt and pepper in a large bowl and mix together well. When the prawns are done, add them to the bowl and toss gently until the butter is melted and the prawns are nicely coated. Serve the prawns right out of the bowl, with another big bowl on the side for the shells.

HALIBUT STEAKS WITH FRESH TOMATO-MINT CHUTNEY

A firm-textured white fish with a large flake, halibut has a delicate flavour that calls for relatively light preparation, so here we pair it with a range of light, bright, citrus flavours. This is a very adaptable approach, which means that if you can't find halibut, you can substitute other white-fleshed fish such as haddock, hake, or cod in this recipe.

Serves 4

THE FISH

4 tbsp freshly cracked coriander seeds
2 tsp freshly cracked white pepper
1 tbsp kosher salt
4 halibut steaks, 225–280g (8–10oz) each, about 2.5cm (1in) thick
2 tbsp olive oil

THE CHUTNEY

2 ripe tomatoes, each about the size of a tennis ball, cored and diced medium
¼ of a medium cucumber, diced medium
Juice of 2 lemons (about 120ml/4fl oz)
4 tbsp roughly chopped fresh mint
2 tbsp peeled and finely chopped fresh ginger
1 tbsp sesame oil
1 tbsp finely chopped fresh chilli pepper of your choice
Kosher salt and freshly cracked black pepper to taste

Build a fire in your grill. When the coals are all ignited, the flames have died down, and the temperature is medium-hot (see p34), you're ready to cook.

Combine the coriander, white pepper, and salt in a small bowl and mix well. Rub the halibut with the oil and coat with the coriander mixture, pressing gently so it adheres. Put the fish on the grill directly over the coals and cook until it is just opaque throughout (5–6 minutes per side). To check for doneness, poke the fish with your finger to test its firmness (see p37); if you're unsure, make a cut in one of the steaks to be sure it is just opaque all the way through.

While the fish is on the grill, combine the chutney ingredients in a small bowl and toss until well-mixed.

Arrange the halibut steaks on a serving plate, top each one with a spoonful of the chutney, and serve, passing the remaining chutney on the side.

SCALLOP COCKTAIL

This is a take on ceviche, the classic Latin American dish in which fish is "cooked" by marinating it in citrus juice. Here we lightly grill the scallops before putting them in the lime environment, which they take to like – well, like a fish to water. To make a more substantial appetizer, we add tomato, avocado, and hearts of palm. This would also make a very delicious and cooling summer lunch for you and a friend.

Serves 4 as an appetizer

THE SALAD

3 tbsp cumin seeds

1 tennis ball-sized tomato, cored and diced small

1 ripe but firm avocado, stoned, peeled, and diced small, and lightly coated with fresh lemon juice

85g (3oz) hearts of palm, sliced 5mm (¼in) thick

½ head cos lettuce, cut crossways into thin strips

THE DRESSING

Juice of 3 limes (about 6 tbsp)

4 tbsp extra virgin olive oil

2 tbsp finely chopped fresh chilli pepper of your choice

2 tbsp roughly chopped fresh oregano

1 tsp finely chopped fresh garlic

Kosher salt and freshly cracked black pepper to taste

THE SCALLOPS

450g (1lb) large sea scallops (about 16), cleaned

2 tbsp vegetable oil

1 tbsp ground cumin

Kosher salt and freshly cracked black pepper to taste

On the hob, toast the cumin seeds in a dry frying pan over a medium heat, shaking frequently to avoid burning, until fragrant and just a shade darker (2–3 minutes). Crack them in a pestle and mortar or with the base of a heavy pan.

Build a fire in your grill. When the coals are all ignited, the flames have died down, and the temperature is medium (*see p34*), you're ready to cook.

Put the tomato, avocado, and hearts of palm in a large bowl; set aside. Combine the lime juice, olive oil, chillies, oregano, garlic, and salt and pepper in a small bowl, and whisk until well-blended. Set aside.

Rub the scallops with the vegetable oil and sprinkle them with the cumin and salt and pepper to taste. Put them on the grill directly over the coals and cook until they are just opaque throughout (3–4 minutes per side). To check for doneness, make a cut in one of the largest scallops to be sure it is opaque all the way through.

Transfer the cooked scallops to the bowl with the tomato mixture. Whisk the dressing again to blend, add just enough to moisten the scallops and vegetables, and toss until evenly coated.

To serve, divide the lettuce among four salad plates, spoon a quarter of the scallop mixture on top of each, and sprinkle with the toasted cumin seeds.

MOROCCO: THE CHARMS OF THE COAST

If you had to pick the most well-known image of Morocco, it would be of the Djemaa el Fna, the kaleidoscopic central square of Marrakech. At night, especially, it is ablaze with excitement: the calls of snake charmers and water sellers, the sparkling robes of magicians, the jostling of huge crowds, and everywhere the smoke of grilling fires. But Morocco has a more tranquil side.

In little-known Rabat, the country's capital and administrative hub, things are very different. In fact, this rather sedate city is not a place we would have stopped at by design. But a number of years ago we ended up spending several days there waiting to get visas to enter Algeria (rather difficult to come by at the time, since the two countries were engaged in a border skirmish). Over the course of our visit, we slowly became enamoured of the gentle graces of the city – the spacious boulevards and gardens, the art deco mansions in the colonial quarter, the grand Mausoleum of Mohammed V, the small but suitably exotic medina. This was a city for strolling, free of the frenetic traffic and relentless touts that can make Marrakech and Fez difficult to negotiate. Best of all, though, were the waterfront restaurants. Our particular favourite was a modest place, about a dozen tables set in single file along the sea, with brilliant fuchsia bougainvillea climbing the cracked walls. It was there that we first discovered *charmoula*. Draped across a procession of super-fresh fish that had spent just the proper amount of time on a charcoal-fired grill, this classic, slightly aggressive herb sauce was the ideal complement to the sweetish, lightly smoky seafood. We returned each afternoon to sit in the sun, listen to the waves, and learn from the masters how fish and strong tastes can perform perfectly together.

MOROCCAN SCALLOPS

The green herb sauce in this dish is our spin on Moroccan *charmoula*, which is typically served with seafood. We love it not just because it's delicious, but also because it's a perfect example of how strong, aggressive flavours can match up very well with seafood, promoting the subtle flavour of the fish rather than overpowering it. To expand the concept, we enliven the large sea scallops we use here with a cumin-coriander crust.

Serves 4

900g (2lb) large sea scallops (about 24 scallops)
4 tbsp olive oil
2 tbsp cumin seeds
1 tbsp ground coriander
1 tbsp paprika
Kosher salt and freshly cracked black pepper
  to taste

For the sauce:
30g (1oz) roughly chopped fresh coriander
4 tbsp roughly chopped fresh parsley
4 tbsp extra virgin olive oil
2 tbsp red wine vinegar
3 garlic cloves, peeled
1 tsp chilli pepper flakes

Build a fire in your grill. When the coals are all ignited, the fire has died down, and the temperature is hot (*see p34*), you're ready to cook.

Combine all of the sauce ingredients in a food processor or blender and purée until smooth. Transfer to a serving bowl and set aside.

Combine the scallops, olive oil, cumin, coriander, paprika, and salt and pepper in a large bowl; toss gently until the scallops are evenly coated with the other ingredients. Put the scallops on the grill over the coals and cook until just opaque throughout (3–4 minutes per side). To check for doneness, cut into one of the scallops to be sure it is just opaque all the way through.

To serve, divide the scallops among 4 plates and drizzle with the sauce. Pass the remaining sauce on the side.

GRILLED MONKFISH WITH CRAB MEAT, CRISPY PARMA HAM, AND ARTICHOKE HEARTS

Mild-flavoured grilled monkfish provides the perfect foil for a trio of Italian ingredients with deep, rich flavours — mellow crab meat, crisp, salty ham, and delicately nutty artichoke hearts. If you have the time and the inclination, fresh artichoke hearts are particularly tasty (see Grilled Artichoke, Rocket, and Radicchio Salad on p258 for how to prepare them), but bottled ones work well here, too.

Serves 4

THE INGREDIENTS

4 monkfish fillets, about 225g (8oz) each
2 tbsp vegetable oil
Kosher salt and freshly cracked black pepper
12 thin slices Parma ham
4 bottled or cooked fresh artichoke hearts, quartered
225g (8oz) fresh white crab meat, carefully picked over
Juice of 1 lemon (about 4 tbsp)
4 tbsp roughly chopped fresh parsley
3 tbsp extra virgin olive oil

Build a fire in your grill. When the coals are all ignited, the flames have died down, and the temperature is medium-hot (*see p34*), you're ready to cook.

Rub the monkfish with the vegetable oil and sprinkle it generously with salt and pepper. Put it on the grill directly over the coals and cook until just opaque throughout (6–8 minutes per side). To check for doneness, poke the fish with your finger to test its firmness (*see p37*); if you're unsure, make a cut in one of the fillets to be sure it is just opaque all the way through.

Meanwhile, put the Parma ham on the grill around the edge of the fire and cook until it starts to brown and crisp at the edges (about 1 minute per side).

Put the artichoke hearts and crab meat in a medium bowl and sprinkle with the lemon juice, parsley, and extra virgin olive oil. Add salt and pepper to taste, and toss gently to blend.

Arrange the fish fillets on a serving plate, spoon the crab mixture on top, crumble the Parma ham over the crab, and serve immediately.

CUMIN SALMON WITH CUCUMBER-CHILLI SALSA

Earthy cumin makes a really nice combination with salmon, which has enough flavour of its own to stand up to the spice. Using seeds rather than powdered cumin also gives you a crunchy crust that's a lovely contrast with the tender fish. This recipe was perfected by East Coast Grill chef Jason Lord at his famed Latin Sunday brunch. The summery salsa is also delicious with any other flavourful fish, such as bluefish, tuna, or even sardines.

Serves 4

THE FISH

4 salmon fillets, skin-on, about 225g (8oz) each
2 tbsp olive oil
2 tbsp cumin seeds, freshly cracked
Kosher salt and freshly cracked black pepper to taste

THE SALSA

½ cucumber, diced small
115g (4oz) mild green chilli peppers (or use less or more to taste)
4 tbsp roughly chopped fresh coriander
Juice of 2 limes (about 4 tbsp)
1 tsp ground cumin
1 tsp ground coriander
1 tsp chilli powder
Kosher salt and freshly cracked black pepper to taste

Build a fire in your grill. When the coals are all ignited, the fire has died down, and the temperature is medium (*see p34*), you're ready to cook.

Rub the salmon fillets on both sides with oil and coat them generously with cumin and salt and pepper, pressing gently to be sure the seasonings adhere. Put the fillets on the grill skin-side down and cook, turning once, until they are just opaque throughout (6–8 minutes per side). To check for doneness, poke the fish with your finger to test its firmness (*see p37*); if you're unsure, cut into one of the fillets at its thickest point to be sure it is opaque all the way through.

While the salmon is on the grill, combine the salsa ingredients in a bowl and toss gently to combine.

Transfer the fillets to a serving plate, top each with a spoonful of salsa, and pass the remaining salsa on the side.

GRILLED MUSSELS WITH MANGO CURRY SAUCE

Mussels are wonderful on the grill, not only because the smoky flavour really enlivens them, but also because they are self-timing: when they open, they're done. We like to complement that grill-ready aspect of these tasty molluscs by making the sauce for them in a pan set right on the grill. This is an ideal appetizer to serve to your guests while you're cooking the main course, since you never have to leave your place at the grill.

Serves 4–6 as an appetizer

THE INGREDIENTS

115g (4oz) unsalted butter, softened

1 tbsp good-quality curry powder

1 tbsp peeled and finely chopped fresh ginger

120ml (4fl oz) mango juice (or substitute equal parts
   orange juice and pineapple juice)

1 tbsp finely chopped fresh chilli peppers of your choice

2kg (4½lb) mussels (about 45–50), scrubbed and bearded

4 slices of good French bread, about 2.5cm (1in) thick

Juice of 2 limes (about 4 tbsp)

4 tbsp roughly chopped fresh coriander

Kosher salt and freshly cracked black pepper to taste

Light a fire well over to one side of your grill (*see p31*), using enough coals to fill a shoebox. When the coals are all ignited, the flames have died down, and the temperature is hot (*see p34*), you're ready to cook.

Make the sauce: put the butter, curry powder, and ginger in a shallow foil tray that is large enough to hold all the mussels and sturdy enough to withstand the heat of the fire. Place the tray on the grill near the fire – not directly over it – and cook for about 2 minutes, stirring a few times, until the butter is melted and the mixture is fragrant. Add the mango juice and chillies, let the sauce come to a simmer, then slide the tray to the side of the grill away from the fire.

Put the mussels directly on the grill grid on the hot side of the grill and cook until they pop open (6–8 minutes). Use tongs to transfer the mussels to the tray with the sauce as they are done. (Discard any that do not open.)

While the mussels are cooking, arrange the bread slices around the perimeter of the fire and cook until lightly toasted—about 2 minutes per side.

When all the mussels are in the pan, stir them around a bit to coat with the sauce and sprinkle with the lime juice, coriander, and salt and pepper. Serve them right out of the pan, along with the toasted bread to soak up the juices.

ROLL-YOUR-OWN PRAWN TACOS
WITH CHILLI SAUCE

For years, these Mexican-inspired tacos have been among the favourite dishes at Chris's East Coast Grill. Three reasons: people love prawns, they love Mexican flavours, and – perhaps most importantly – they love putting together their own meal. So when you set up the prawn taco bar in your garden, you're going to be a very popular host.

Serves 4 as an appetizer

THE PRAWNS

450g (1lb) prawns, 16/20 size, peeled, tails removed
2 tbsp olive oil
1 tbsp chilli powder
Salt and freshly cracked black pepper to taste

THE SAUCE

30g (1oz) dried chillies, steeped in hot water for 40 minutes, drained, and puréed in a blender
1 tsp ground cumin
Juice of 2 limes (about 4 tbsp)
Kosher salt and freshly cracked black pepper to taste

THE GARNISHES

1 ripe but firm avocado, peeled, stoned, diced small, and lightly coated with fresh lemon juice
½ small red onion, peeled and thinly sliced
115g (4oz) green cabbage, shredded
4 tbsp roughly chopped fresh coriander
1 large tomato, diced
2 slices peeled fresh pineapple, about 1cm (½in) thick
1 tbsp olive oil
Salt and freshly cracked black pepper to taste

THE WRAPS

8 corn or flour tortillas, 15–20cm (6–8in) diameter

Build a fire in your grill. When the coals are all ignited, the flames have died down, and the temperature is hot (*see p34*), you're ready to cook.

Put all the garnish ingredients except the pineapple, oil, and salt and pepper in separate small bowls, arrange the bowls on a serving plate, then cover and set aside until serving time. Combine the sauce ingredients in a small bowl.

Rub the pineapple slices with olive oil, sprinkle with salt and pepper, and grill until golden-brown and slightly charred (3–4 minutes per side). Dice the pineapple, put it in a small serving bowl, and cover to keep warm.

Rub the prawns with olive oil and sprinkle with the chilli powder and plenty of salt and pepper. Put them on the grill directly over the coals and cook until just opaque throughout (3–4 minutes each side). To check for doneness, make a cut in one and peek in. Halve the prawns if desired, put in a serving bowl, and cover loosely to keep warm.

Put the tortillas on the grill to toast briefly, flipping every 10 seconds or so, until they are soft and pliable (about 1 minute). Wrap the stack of warm tortillas in a large napkin or foil, and bring them to the table along with the prawns, the sauce, and the plate of garnishes so your guests can "roll their own".

SWORDFISH WITH TOMATO-RAISIN RELISH

It's fun to make things at home that you usually buy from a shop; the difference is amazing. Here we make a raisin and dried tomato relish using the simple technique of letting the fruit (and, yes, tomatoes are fruits) sit in a low oven for up to 10 hours. You'll love the plush texture and clean flavours they bring to the relish, which is a beautiful complement to meaty grilled swordfish.

Serves 4

THE FISH

4 swordfish steaks, 225g (8oz) each, about 2.5cm (1in) thick
2 tbsp olive oil
2 tbsp coriander seeds, freshly cracked
Kosher salt and freshly cracked black pepper

THE RELISH

6 plum tomatoes, cored and cut in half
2 tbsp olive oil
200g (7oz) seedless green grapes
4 tbsp extra virgin olive oil
2 tbsp roughly chopped fresh oregano
1 tbsp dry sherry
1 tsp finely chopped fresh garlic
Pinch chilli pepper flakes
Kosher salt and freshly cracked black pepper to taste

Dry the fruits for the relish: preheat the oven to 110°C (225°F/Gas ¼). Rub the tomato halves with the 2 tbsp of ordinary olive oil and place them cut-side up on a wire rack set over a baking sheet. Put the grapes on the rack beside the tomatoes, and place the baking sheet on the middle shelf of the oven. Remove the grapes when they resemble plump raisins (4–6 hours). Return the tomatoes to the oven and leave them until they are reduced in size by about one-quarter and shrivelled on the outside but still tender and juicy inside (2–4 hours more). Cut each dried tomato half in half again.

Combine the dried grapes and tomatoes in a medium bowl along with the extra virgin olive oil, oregano, sherry, garlic, chilli flakes, and salt and pepper and mix well.

Build a fire in your grill. When the coals are all ignited, the flames have died down, and the temperature is hot (*see p34*), you're ready to cook.

Rub the swordfish steaks with oil and sprinkle them generously with coriander, salt, and pepper, pressing gently to be sure the seasonings adhere. Put the fish on the grill directly over the coals and cook until it is just opaque throughout (5–7 minutes per side). To check for doneness, poke the fish with your finger to test its firmness (*see p37*); if you're unsure, cut into a steak at its thickest point to be sure it is just opaque all the way through.

Arrange the swordfish steaks on a serving plate, top each with a spoonful of relish, and pass the remaining relish on the side.

HAWAIIAN TUNA
WITH QUICK CUCUMBER-SESAME RELISH

At one point in my rather aimless youth, I (Chris) spent some time surfing – and occasionally working in restaurant kitchens – in Lahaina on the Hawaiian island of Maui. I ate a lot of poke, a raw fish dish that is a traditional Hawaiian snack. This is a variation on that theme, in which we sear tuna hard on the outside, then mix it with traditional poke flavours. Because the fish spends only a short time over the flames, when you cut into it you'll get some sear and some raw in each bite – a great combination.

Serves 4 as an appetizer

THE FISH

3 tbsp sesame seeds
1 super-fresh tuna steak, about 450g (1lb) in weight and about 5cm (2in) thick
2 tbsp sesame oil
2 tbsp freshly cracked white pepper
2 tbsp freshly cracked coriander seeds (or substitute 1 tbsp ground coriander)
1 tbsp kosher salt
3 spring onions, including green tops, finely chopped

THE RELISH

1 cucumber, peeled and deseeded if desired, diced small
3 tbsp sesame oil
Juice of 1 lime (about 2 tbsp)
2 tbsp peeled and finely chopped fresh ginger
1 tbsp granulated sugar
Kosher salt to taste

Build a fire in your grill. When the coals are all ignited, the fire has died down, and the temperature is hot (*see p34*), you're ready to cook.

Meanwhile, on the hob, toast the sesame seeds in a dry frying pan over a medium heat, shaking frequently to avoid burning, until they are fragrant and just a shade darker (3–5 minutes). Set them aside.

Combine the relish ingredients in a medium bowl; mix well and divide among 4 salad plates.

Cut the tuna steak into four 5cm (2in) cubes, and put them into a bowl. Drizzle the tuna with the sesame oil, add the pepper, coriander, and salt, and toss gently to coat. Place the tuna on the hottest part of the grill and sear until you have a dark brown, crispy crust on at least 2 sides (3–4 minutes per side). You're aiming for a dark, crusty exterior, and a cool, raw centre.

Transfer the fish to a cutting board, slice it thin, and fan the slices out beside the cucumber relish on each plate. Garnish with the toasted sesame seeds and spring onions and serve.

GRILLED LEMON-PEPPER MACKEREL
WITH TOMATO-GREEN OLIVE RELISH

Full-flavoured, rich, and distinct, the mackerel is one of our favourite fish, with plenty of character to stand up to the grill flavour. The relish we serve with the mackerel here has Portuguese overtones, in tribute to the sardines we had on a beach in the Algarve many years ago (*see p96*), which convinced us of the virtues of grilling rich-flavoured fish.

Serves 4

THE FISH

4 mackerel fillets, about 225g (8oz) each (or substitute fillets of bluefish, pompano, or salmon)
2 tbsp olive oil

THE RUB

2 tbsp freshly cracked black pepper
1 tbsp finely chopped lemon zest
½ tsp ground ginger
Kosher salt to taste

THE RELISH

1 tbsp cumin seed (or 1½ tsp ground cumin)
2 ripe tomatoes, cored and diced large
85g (3oz) roughly chopped pitted green olives
4 tbsp extra virgin olive oil
4 tbsp roughly chopped fresh parsley
4 tbsp roughly chopped fresh mint
2 tsp drained capers
Kosher salt and freshly cracked black pepper

If using whole cumin seeds in the relish, toast them on the hob in a frying pan over a medium-high heat until they are fragrant and just a shade darker (3–5 minutes). Set them aside.

Build a fire in your grill. When the coals are all ignited, the fire has died down, and the temperature is medium (*see p34*), you're ready to cook.

While the coals are heating up, make the relish: combine the cumin, tomatoes, olives, olive oil, parsley, mint, and capers in a medium bowl and mix well. Season to taste with salt and pepper, and transfer to a serving dish.

Now make the rub: combine the black pepper, lemon zest, ginger, and salt in a small bowl and mix well.

Rub the mackerel fillets all over with the olive oil and then coat with the spice rub, pressing gently to be sure it adheres. Put the fillets on the grill over the coals and cook until they are nicely seared on the outside and just opaque on the inside (4–6 minutes per side). To check for doneness, manipulate one of the fillets so you can see inside it at its thickest point to be sure it is just opaque all the way through.

Serve each fillet topped with a spoonful of relish, and pass the remaining relish on the side.

CLAMS IN CHILLI-BUTTER SAUCE

This is a variation on Clams Johnson, a dish invented in the late 1980s by our friend Steve Johnson, now the chef/owner of the Rendezvous restaurant in Cambridge, Massachusetts. We like digging clams along the Massachusetts coast, and this is a great way to cook them. Like mussels, they take well to the smoky flavour of the grill and have the added advantage of letting you know when they're cooked, because they pop open. You can also serve these over pasta, if you like.

Serves 4 as an appetizer

THE INGREDIENTS

115g (4oz) unsalted butter, softened
120ml (4fl oz) dry white wine
1 tbsp finely chopped garlic
1 tsp chilli pepper flakes
32 clams, scrubbed
4 slices of good French bread, about 2.5cm (1in) thick
4 tbsp roughly chopped fresh parsley
Kosher salt and freshly cracked black pepper to taste

Light a fire well over to one side of your grill, using enough coals to fill a shoebox. When the coals are all ignited, the flames have died down, and the temperature is hot (*see p34*), you're ready to cook.

Put the butter, wine, garlic, and red pepper flakes in a shallow foil tray that is large enough to hold all the clams in a single layer and sturdy enough to resist the heat of the fire. Place the tray on the grill near the fire, not directly over it, and cook for about 2 minutes, stirring a few times, until the butter is melted and the mixture is fragrant. Let the sauce come to a simmer, then slide the pan over to the side of the grill away from the fire.

Place the clams on the hot side of the grill, directly on the grill grate, and cook them until they pop open (8–10 minutes). Use tongs to transfer the clams to the tray containing the sauce as they are done. (Discard any clams that do not open.)

While the clams are cooking, arrange the bread slices around the perimeter of the fire and grill until lightly toasted (about 2 minutes per side).

When all the clams are in the tray, stir them around a bit to coat with the sauce, and sprinkle generously with parsley and salt and pepper. Serve them right out of the tray, along with the toasted bread to soak up the juices.

GRILLED BLUEFISH WITH EXOTIC SPICES AND MIRIN-MUSTARD SAUCE

The Japanese are, of course, masters of seafood, and have a particularly deft way with strong-flavoured ingredients like eel and mackerel. Here we pair a sweet and pungent Japanese-style sauce with bluefish, another fish with a somewhat aggressive flavour. To add to the party, we coat the fish with a home-made five-spice powder before it goes over the flames. While you're at it, you might double or triple the quantities for the spice rub, just to have some extra on hand for rubbing on other fish for the grill. If bluefish is not available, substitute salmon or mackerel.

Serves 4

THE FISH

4 bluefish fillets, about 225g (8oz) each, or substitute salmon or mackerel
2 tbsp sesame oil
Kosher salt and freshly cracked black pepper

THE SPICE RUB

1 tsp ground ginger
1 tsp ground white pepper
1 tsp ground coriander
Pinch of ground cinnamon
Pinch of ground cardamom

THE SAUCE

4 tbsp Dijon mustard
60ml (2fl oz) mirin (sweet rice wine)
2 tbsp rice vinegar
2 tbsp sesame oil
2 tbsp finely chopped spring onions
Kosher salt and freshly cracked black pepper to taste

Build a fire in your grill. When the coals are all ignited, the fire has died down, and the temperature is medium (*see p34*), you're ready to cook.

Combine the spice rub ingredients in a small bowl and mix well.

Rub the fish fillets with sesame oil, sprinkle with salt and pepper, then coat them generously with the spice rub, pressing gently to be sure it adheres. Put the fillets on the grill over the coals, skin-side up, and cook until just opaque all the way through (6–8 minutes per side). To check for doneness, poke the fish with your finger to test its firmness (*see p37*); if you're unsure, cut into one of the fillets at its thickest point to be sure it is just opaque all the way through.

While the fish cooks, make the sauce: whisk the mustard, mirin, vinegar, sesame oil, and spring onions together in a small bowl; season to taste with salt and pepper.

Serve the bluefish drizzled with mustard sauce, and pass any remaining sauce on the side.

THAI GRILLED PRAWNS

Prawns are a breeze on the grill — quick, easy, and very tasty. The main thing you have to do is be sure you don't overcook them; as soon as they are just opaque all the way through, take them off the fire. Here we combine them with a range of Thai flavours, including the classic herb trio of mint, basil, and coriander, for a quick but superflavourful appetizer.

Serves 4 as an appetizer

THE INGREDIENTS

450g (1lb) king prawns, peeled, but with tails intact
2 tbsp olive oil
Kosher salt and freshly cracked white pepper
1 recipe Chilli-Fish Sauce Relish (*see p115*)
1 tbsp roughly chopped fresh mint
1 tbsp roughly chopped fresh Thai basil
   (or substitute Italian basil)
1 tbsp roughly chopped fresh coriander

Build a fire in your grill. When the coals are all ignited, the flames have died down, and the temperature is hot (*see p34*), you're ready to cook.

Rub the prawns with oil, sprinkle generously with salt and white pepper, then put them on the grill directly over the coals and cook until they are just cooked through (3–4 minutes per side). To check for doneness, poke the prawns with your finger to test their firmness (*see p37*); if you're unsure, make a cut in one of the prawns at its thickest point to be sure it is just opaque all the way through.

Transfer the prawns to a large bowl, add the Chilli-Fish Sauce Relish, and toss gently until the prawns are well-coated. Add the mint, basil, and coriander and toss again. Divide the prawns among four plates and serve.

THINGS WITH WINGS

CHICKEN, THAT MOST EVERYDAY OF MODERN FOWL, TAKES ON A WHOLE NEW FLAVOUR WHEN COOKED OVER THE SMOKY HEAT OF A CHARCOAL FIRE. SLIGHTLY MORE EXOTIC BIRDS, FROM DUCK TO QUAIL TO SQUAB, ALSO COME INTO THEIR OWN OVER THE GRILL. MATCHED WITH FLAVOURS FROM AROUND THE WORLD, THEY'RE IRRESISTIBLE.

ZESTY CHICKEN BREAST WITH PLUM AND GINGER SAUCE

We love combining fruit and meat, and this approach works very well with poultry, too. We leave the plums in this sauce rather chunky, because it creates more textural contrast between the interior and exterior of the fruit; but for a somewhat more elegant sauce, you can also just purée the mixture once it's cooked. If good-quality plums aren't available, feel free to substitute apricots, peaches, or even mangoes.

Serves 4

THE CHICKEN

4 boneless skin-on chicken breasts, 300–350g (10–12oz) each
3 tbsp olive oil
Kosher salt and freshly cracked black pepper
4 tbsp finely chopped orange zest

THE SAUCE

2 tbsp olive oil
1 medium red onion, peeled and diced small
3 ripe plums, stoned and quartered
1 tbsp peeled and finely chopped fresh ginger
Juice of 1 lemon (about 4 tbsp)
5 tbsp roughly chopped fresh parsley
Kosher salt and freshly cracked black pepper to taste

Build a fire in your grill. When the coals are all ignited, the flames have died down, and the temperature is medium (see p34), you're ready to cook.

Rub the chicken breasts with the oil and sprinkle them generously with salt and pepper and the orange zest, pressing gently so it adheres. Put the chicken on the grill directly over the coals, skin-side down, and cook, turning once, until they are opaque all the way through (7–9 minutes per side). To check for doneness, poke the chicken with your finger to test its firmness (see p37); if you're unsure, make a small cut in the thickest part of one piece to be sure there is no pinkness in the centre.

While the chicken is cooking, make the sauce: on the hob, heat the oil in a large sauté pan over a medium-high heat until hot but not smoking. Add the onions and sauté, stirring occasionally, until golden-brown (11–13 minutes). Add the plums and ginger and cook, stirring frequently, for another 3 minutes, or until the plums are tender but not mushy. Remove from the heat, stir in the lemon juice and parsley, and add salt and pepper to taste.

Serve the chicken hot, with a spoonful of plum sauce on each portion. Pass the remaining sauce on the side.

GRILLED DUCK BREAST WITH ORANGE-CARDAMOM GLAZE

Here's a twist on the French classic duck à l'orange, but a lot easier and a little more exotic, with subtly aromatic cardamom and the subdued bite of ginger added to the sweet-tart of the orange. This is a great dish to serve when you want something a little fancy but don't want to spend a whole lot of time cooking.

Serves 4

THE DUCK

4 boneless duck breasts, 300–350g (10–12oz) each, skin-on, with most of the fat removed

2 tbsp olive oil

Kosher salt and freshly cracked black pepper

THE GLAZE

240ml (8fl oz) orange juice

240ml (8fl oz) red wine

2 tbsp peeled and finely chopped fresh ginger

1 tbsp finely chopped orange zest

2 green cardamom pods, lightly cracked

2 tbsp soft dark brown sugar

Kosher salt and freshly cracked black pepper to taste

Build a fire in your grill. When the coals are all ignited, the flames have died down, and the temperature is medium (*see p34*), you're ready to cook.

Combine the glaze ingredients in a small saucepan and bring to the boil on the hob over a medium heat, stirring occasionally. Adjust the heat so the mixture just simmers gently, and cook until it has been reduced by about two-thirds (25–30 minutes). Remove from the heat and set it aside.

Rub the duck breasts with the oil, sprinkle them generously with salt and pepper, and arrange them skin-side down on the grill, off to the edge of the coals. Cook the duck slowly, allowing the fat to drip off at an even pace and giving the skin time to crisp (6–8 minutes per side). If fat drips into the fire and causes flare-ups, move the duck breasts so they are not directly over the flames. During the last minute of cooking, brush them liberally with the glaze. When the duck is nicely browned, check for doneness by poking the meat with your finger to test its firmness (*see p37*); if you're unsure, make a small cut in the thickest part of one breast; it should be slightly less done than you like (we prefer them medium-rare).

Serve, passing the remaining glaze on the side.

FLAVOUR FOOTPRINT INDIA

From the lentil and rice dishes of Gujarat to the tandoor cooking of the Punjab and the fiery lamb dishes of Andhra Pradesh, the cuisines of India are at least as varied as those of Europe. All, however, are characterized by the expert use of a wide variety of spices, very often used whole, and frequently combined into signature spice mixes called masalas. The five recipes here provide a quick primer on the way spices can add powerful excitement to everyday food without much effort.

All-Purpose Indian Masala Rub
Makes about 115g (4oz)

This complex dry spice rub is excellent rubbed on steaks, chops of any variety, or chicken before grilling.

4 tbsp coriander seeds
2 tbsp cumin seeds
2 tbsp yellow mustard seeds
2 tbsp fennel seeds
2 tbsp white peppercorns
2 small dried red chillies
2 tbsp kosher salt
1 tbsp ground ginger
1 tbsp ground turmeric

Combine the coriander seeds, cumin seeds, mustard seeds, fennel seeds, peppercorns, and chillies in a dry frying pan over a medium-high heat and toast until fragrant (3–4 minutes), shaking the pan frequently. Remove from the heat and cool to room temperature. Transfer to a spice mill or clean coffee grinder, add the salt, ginger, and turmeric, and grind to a coarse powder. Stored in an airtight container and kept in a cool, dark place, this dry rub will last for months.

Curry-Mint Paste
Makes about 85g (3oz)

Use this as a last-minute rub before lamb, chicken, or pork go on the grill, or as a quick marinade (up to 3 hours before cooking).

30g (1oz) fresh mint leaves
15g (½oz) fresh coriander leaves
2 tbsp curry powder
2 tbsp vegetable oil
1 tbsp finely chopped fresh ginger
1 tbsp kosher salt

Combine all the ingredients in a small bowl or, if you prefer a finer paste, mash in a mortar and pestle. This will last, covered and refrigerated, for 2–3 days.

All-Purpose Indian Masala Rub

Fresh Coconut Relish
Makes about 200g (7oz)

This is perfect with fish fillets or chicken breasts.

115g (4oz) grated fresh coconut
Juice of 2 limes (about 4 tbsp)
4 tbsp roughly chopped fresh coriander
2 tbsp roughly chopped fresh green chilli pepper of
   your choice
1 tbsp peeled and finely chopped fresh ginger
1 tsp granulated sugar
Kosher salt and freshly cracked black pepper to taste

Combine all the ingredients in a small bowl and
mix well. This relish will keep, covered and
refrigerated, for 2–3 days.

Spicy Tomato Relish
Makes about 340g (12oz)

Put out a bowl of this whenever you are serving
smaller pieces of fish, chicken, or pork.

1 ripe tomato, cored and diced small
85g (3oz) diced cucumber
5 tbsp roughly chopped fresh coriander
Juice of 1 lemon (about 4 tbsp)
2 tbsp finely chopped fresh green chilli pepper of your choice
1 tbsp brown mustard seeds
1 tsp ground cumin
Kosher salt and freshly cracked black pepper to taste

Combine all the ingredients in a medium bowl
and mix well. This relish will keep, covered and
refrigerated, for 3–4 days.

**SIGNATURE INGREDIENTS/TOP ROW (LEFT TO
RIGHT)** Turmeric, cardamom, fennel seeds, mustard seeds;
SECOND ROW Lime, cumin seeds, ginger, mint; **THIRD
ROW** Saffron, tamarind, coconut, fenugreek; **BOTTOM ROW**
Fresh coriander, chillies, coriander seed, garlic.

Dried Apricot Chutney
Makes about 400g (14oz)

This is great to make in the winter, when it's hard to
find good-quality fresh fruit. Try it with pork, lamb, or
in fact any roasted meat.

2 tbsp olive oil
½ small red onion, peeled and diced small
180g (6oz) roughly chopped dried apricots
1 tbsp peeled and finely chopped fresh ginger
1 tbsp finely chopped fresh chilli pepper of your choice
60ml (2fl oz) fresh orange juice
60ml (2fl oz) red wine vinegar
Juice of 1 lime (about 2 tbsp)
Kosher salt and freshly cracked black pepper to taste

Heat the oil in a sauté pan over a medium-high heat
until hot but not smoking. Add the onions and sauté,
stirring occasionally, until transparent (7–9 minutes).
Add the apricots, ginger, and chilli pepper, and cook,
stirring frequently, until fragrant (about 2 minutes
more). Add the orange juice and vinegar and mix well.
Bring to a simmer, adjust the heat to low, and cook
gently, stirring frequently, until the mixture thickens –
about 10 minutes. Remove from the heat and let cool
slightly. Add the lime juice and mix well. This chutney
will keep, covered and refrigerated, for about a week.

Spicy Tomato Relish

QUAIL WITH CHILLI-PEANUT SAUCE

We love quail, not only because they're delicious but also because you can pick them up and eat them with your fingers even in polite company. They are also great for grilling, since they cook quickly and the sear and smoke complements the rather delicate flavour of the bird. We like to pair them with rather strongly flavoured sauces – like those in the Mexican-inspired *mole* made with dried ancho chilli peppers that accompanies them here.

Serves 8 as an appetizer, 4 as a main course

THE QUAIL

8 quail, either semi-boneless or butterflied with the backbone removed
2 tbsp olive oil
Kosher salt and freshly cracked black pepper
4 tbsp roughly chopped fresh coriander
Juice of 1 lime (about 2 tbsp)

THE SAUCE

4 dried ancho chilli peppers, seeded and stemmed
3 tbsp olive oil
1 small red onion, peeled and diced small
4 tbsp roasted unsalted peanuts
2 tbsp finely chopped fresh garlic
½ a tennis ball-sized tomato, cored and chopped
5 tbsp distilled white vinegar
2 tbsp orange juice
1 tsp ground cumin
1 tsp ground coriander
Pinch of cinnamon
Kosher salt and freshly cracked black pepper to taste

Build a fire in your grill. When the coals are all ignited, the flames have died down, and the temperature is medium-hot (*see p34*), you're ready to cook.

For the sauce: on the hob, toast the chillies in a small frying pan over a medium heat until fragrant (2–3 minutes); place in a small bowl and cover with boiling water. Let them soak for 40 minutes to rehydrate them, then drain.

Heat the oil in a sauté pan or frying pan over a medium-high heat until hot but not smoking. Add the onion and sauté, stirring occasionally, until transparent (7–9 minutes). Add the peanuts and garlic and sauté, stirring frequently, until fragrant, about 2 minutes more. Stir in the chillies and the tomato, vinegar, orange juice, cumin, coriander, cinnamon, and salt and pepper. Bring to a simmer and cook, stirring occasionally, for 15 minutes. Set aside to cool slightly, then transfer to a blender or food processor and purée. Return the sauce to the sauté pan.

Rub the quails with oil, sprinkle them generously with salt and pepper, then put them on the grill directly over the coals and cook until there is no more than a hint of pink near the bone when you cut into them (4–6 minutes per side). Transfer the quail to a large, shallow serving bowl and cover loosely to keep warm.

Reheat the sauce, thinning with water if necessary. Pour the sauce over the quail, turning to coat; sprinkle with the fresh coriander and lime juice, and serve.

CHICKEN WITH SULTANA VINAIGRETTE

This simple late summer/early autumn recipe pairs chicken with grilled apples – delicious and easy, but still unusual enough in most cooks' repertoires to seem somewhat exotic. Granny Smith apples work well, but if you have a local apple that is firm and a little tart, then use it.

Serves 4

THE CHICKEN

4 bone-in, skin-on split chicken breasts,
  300–350g (10–12oz) each
2 tbsp vegetable oil
Kosher salt and freshly cracked black pepper

THE VINAIGRETTE

5 tbsp extra virgin olive oil
4 tbsp balsamic vinegar
4 tbsp sultanas, finely chopped
2 tbsp finely chopped fresh sage
1 tsp soft dark brown sugar

THE APPLES

2 Granny Smith or other green apples, halved through
  the stem and cored
1 tbsp vegetable oil
Kosher salt and freshly cracked black pepper to taste

Build a multilevel fire in your grill (*see p31*). When the coals are all ignited, the fire has died down, and the temperature is medium (*see p34*), you're ready to cook.

Rub the chicken breasts with vegetable oil, sprinkle generously with salt and pepper, and place them skin-side down on the hottest part of the grill. Cook until the skin is very brown and crisp (about 4 minutes); flip them over and cook on the other side for about 4 minutes more. To finish, move the breasts to the cooler side of the grill, skin-side down, and cover them with an inverted foil tray until they are completely opaque inside but not dried out (10–12 minutes more). To check for doneness, poke the meat with your finger to test its firmness (*see p37*); if you're unsure, cut into the thickest part of the largest breast and check to be sure it is opaque all the way through, with no pinkness near the bone.

While the chicken is cooking, make the vinaigrette: combine the olive oil, vinegar, sultanas, sage, and brown sugar in a bowl large enough to hold at least one of the chicken breasts, whisking until the sugar dissolves. Set aside.

As soon as you move the chicken to the cooler side of the grill, rub the apple halves with vegetable oil, sprinkle them generously with salt and pepper, and arrange them, cut-side down, beside the chicken. Cook the apples until the cut sides are golden-brown (about 5 minutes).

As the chicken breasts are done, dunk them one at a time in the bowl of vinaigrette, then transfer to a serving plate. Arrange the apples around the chicken, drizzle the remaining vinaigrette over all, and serve.

CHILLI-GARLIC CHICKEN WITH LEMONGRASS-GINGER COLE SLAW

If you're pressed for time, you can always make this delicious spice-rubbed chicken without the cole slaw. But the slaw is a great, subtle complement to the robust flavour of the chicken, and the unique aromatic taste of the lemongrass is worth the effort it takes to extract and chop the soft inner core.

Serves 4

THE CHICKEN

3 tbsp sesame oil

2 tbsp finely chopped fresh garlic

2 tbsp finely chopped fresh chilli pepper of your choice

2 tbsp kosher salt

2 tbsp freshly cracked black pepper

4 boneless, skin-on whole chicken breasts, 300–350g (10–12oz) each

THE COLE SLAW

5 tbsp rice wine vinegar

3 tbsp soy sauce

1 tbsp sesame oil

2 tbsp peeled and finely chopped fresh ginger

2 stalks lemongrass, finely chopped (use the tender, inner portion of the bottom third only)

2 tbsp roughly chopped fresh Thai basil (or substitute regular basil)

Juice of 1 lime (about 2 tbsp)

2 tbsp granulated sugar

Kosher salt and freshly cracked black pepper to taste

½ small head Chinese cabbage, cut crossways into thin strips

Build a fire in your grill. When the coals are all ignited, the flames have died down, and the temperature is medium (*see p34*), you're ready to cook.

Combine the sesame oil, garlic, chillies, salt, and pepper in a small bowl and mix well. Rub the chicken breasts with the sesame mixture, place them on the grill, skin-side down, and cook, turning once, until they are opaque all the way through (7–9 minutes per side). To check for doneness, poke the chicken with your finger to test its firmness (*see p37*); if you're unsure, make a small cut in the thickest part of the largest breast to be sure that it is opaque all the way through.

While the chicken is on the grill, combine all of the slaw ingredients except the cabbage in a small bowl and whisk until well-blended. Put the cabbage in a large bowl, add enough dressing to just moisten it, and toss until the cabbage is well-coated. Divide the slaw among 4 plates.

When the chicken is done, transfer the breasts to a cutting board and slice them crossways into strips. Fan the chicken over the slaw on each plate, and drizzle with any remaining dressing.

WEST INDIAN CHICKEN BREASTS
WITH SOUR ORANGE MOJO

In this tribute to the jerk masters of Jamaica's Boston Bay (*see also p162*), a flavourful spice paste forms a super-hot and spicy crust on the outside of tender chicken breasts. It's an ideal dish if you like chicken, but are tired of the usual ways of preparing it. The sourness of the orange mojo provides just the right complement to the fiery chicken; it's also good served alongside just about any other kind of grilled fowl.

Serves 4

THE CHICKEN

4 boneless, skinless whole chicken breasts, 300–350g (10–12oz) each
5 tbsp made yellow mustard
4 Scotch Bonnet chilli peppers, stemmed
1 tbsp peeled and finely chopped fresh ginger
1 tbsp good-quality curry powder
4 tbsp roughly chopped spring onions, white and green parts
Kosher salt and freshly cracked black pepper to taste

THE MOJO

Juice of 2 oranges (about 240ml/8fl oz)
5 tbsp distilled white vinegar
5 tbsp olive oil
2 tbsp roughly chopped fresh oregano
1 tbsp finely chopped fresh garlic
1 tbsp finely chopped fresh chilli pepper of your choice
Kosher salt and freshly cracked black pepper to taste

Place the chicken breasts in a large, shallow bowl. Combine the mustard, chillies, ginger, curry powder, spring onions, and salt and pepper in a blender or food processor and purée; pour over the chicken, turning each piece to coat. Cover and refrigerate for 1 hour, turning once or twice if you remember.

While the chicken marinates, build a fire in your grill. When the coals are all ignited, the flames have died down, and the temperature is medium (*see p34*), you're ready to cook.

Combine all the mojo ingredients in a medium bowl, mix well, and set aside.

Place the chicken breasts on the grill directly over the coals and cook, turning once, until they are opaque all the way through (7–9 minutes per side). To check for doneness, poke the chicken with your finger to test its firmness (*see p37*); if you're unsure, make a small cut in the thickest part of the largest breast to be sure that it is opaque all the way through.

To serve, arrange the chicken breasts on a serving plate and spoon the mojo over them.

CHICKEN DRUMSTICKS WITH ORANGES AND GREEN OLIVES

We think chicken drumsticks are a seriously underrated food: they have much more flavour than the more popular chicken breasts, you can eat them with your fingers, and they are about half the price. For a bit of exotic allure that will hopefully improve their image, we serve them with a Moroccan-inspired mixture of oranges and olives enlivened with lemon juice, garlic, and hot red pepper.

Serves 4

THE INGREDIENTS

2 large oranges
115g (4oz) pitted green olives
Juice of 1½ lemons (about 5 tbsp)
4 tbsp extra virgin olive oil
1 tsp finely chopped fresh garlic
1 tsp chilli pepper flakes
Kosher salt and freshly cracked black pepper
8 chicken drumsticks

Build a fire in your grill. When the coals are all ignited, the flames have died down, and the temperature is medium-low (*see p34*), you're ready to cook.

Use a vegetable peeler to remove the zest from both oranges. Finely chop the zest and set it aside. (You should have about 2 tbsp of zest.) With a sharp knife, remove and discard all of the white pith from the oranges. Working over a medium-sized bowl to catch the juice, cut between the membranes of each orange to remove each segment, taking care to remove any seeds. Add the segments to the juice together with the olives, lemon juice, olive oil, reserved zest, garlic, chilli flakes, and salt and pepper to taste; mix well and set aside.

Sprinkle the drumsticks generously with salt and pepper, then place them on the grill directly over the coals and cook for 12–14 minutes, rolling them around to ensure even browning. To check for doneness, poke the meat with your finger to test its firmness (*see p37*); if you're unsure, cut into the thickest part of the largest drumstick to be sure it's opaque all the way through, with no redness near the bone.

Arrange the drumsticks on a serving plate and spoon the orange-olive mixture over and around them.

JAMAICA: FEELING THE HEAT

After I (Chris) graduated from culinary school, I ran fairly quickly through a number of food industry jobs – private chef on a yacht that rarely left harbour, line cook at a resort in Hawaii, sous-chef at a large hotel in Boston....

I learned something from each of them, but none of them fired my imagination. So eventually I decided to do what any sensible young man would do – quit my job and embark on an epic surfing trip through the Caribbean and South and Central America. It was perhaps the best decision of my life, because it was on this trip that my formal training and my love of intensely flavoured, casual food came together. About a third of the way through the trip, I was lucky enough to spend a series of languorous afternoons (because surfers are nothing if not languorous when the surf isn't up) on the northern coast of Jamaica, near Boston Bay. As any aficionado knows, this is the original home of "jerk" cooking, a unique technique originally developed by runaway slaves called maroons. Jerk involves coating meat (most often chicken or pork) with a spice paste featuring the incendiary Scotch Bonnet chilli pepper, which is among the very hottest in the world, but also has a distinctly floral, aromatic flavour. Once the paste is applied, the food is slowly cooked over a smoky fire, usually fuelled by pimento wood. The guys who hang out around the pits cooking jerk may be the very definition of laid-back, but the food they produce is anything but – it's a smoke-infused, aromatic, blisteringly hot treat. I quickly became addicted. Plus, from watching these guys and eating their food, I learned the virtues of spice pastes. Because they include fresh ingredients such as garlic and fresh chillies, these pastes have even more dynamic flavours than the dry spice rubs I had already begun using. And, really, you can't ask more than that – lazy days in the sun, great food, and a culinary lesson you use for the rest of your life.

JERK WINGS FROM HELL

These super-fiery wings, powered by the outrageous Scotch Bonnet chilli pepper, are one of the most popular snacks for the macho line cooks at Chris's East Coast Grill. When these wings come fresh off the grill, we can practically guarantee you will go for them, even if you're not a chilli aficionado.

Serves 4 as an appetizer

900g (2lb) chicken wings
2 tbsp olive oil
Kosher salt and freshly cracked black pepper
4 tbsp distilled white vinegar
1 large fresh Scotch Bonnet chilli pepper, finely chopped (about 2 tbsp)
2 tbsp American yellow mustard
2 tbsp dried oregano
Kosher salt and freshly cracked black pepper to taste
2 tbsp finely chopped spring onions
1 lime, halved

Build a fire in your grill. When the coals are all ignited, the flames have died down, and the temperature is medium (see p34), you're ready to cook.

Cut each wing into 3 sections. Discard the wing tips or save them for stock.

Rub the wing pieces with the oil, sprinkle them generously with salt and pepper, then put them on the grill directly over the coals and cook, rolling them around regularly to be sure they cook evenly, until they are golden-brown (10–15 minutes). To check for doneness, cut into one to make sure there is no redness near the bone.

While the wings are cooking, combine the vinegar, chilli, mustard, oregano, and salt and pepper in a bowl large enough to hold all of the wings and mix well.

As the wings come off the grill, add them to the bowl of sauce, turning to coat. Sprinkle the wings with the spring onions, squeeze on the lime juice, and serve them right out of the bowl.

HONEY- AND GINGER-GLAZED SQUAB

Game birds are great on the grill because they respond very well to high-heat cooking. This is particularly true of the young, plump pigeons known as squab, which to us have many of the flavour characteristics of beef, including being best served rare.

Serves 4

THE SQUAB

Juice of 1 lemon (about 4 tbsp)
4 tbsp olive oil
2 tbsp peeled and finely chopped fresh ginger
2 tbsp freshly cracked coriander seeds
1 tbsp finely chopped fresh garlic
4 medium squab or pigeons, butterflied
Kosher salt and freshly cracked black pepper

THE GLAZE

4 tbsp honey
2 tbsp roughly chopped fresh mint

1 tbsp peeled and finely chopped fresh ginger
1 tbsp fresh lemon juice
1 tsp chilli pepper flakes

THE GARNISHES

6 thick slices bacon, diced large
5 fresh figs, halved lengthways
1 tbsp olive oil
Kosher salt and freshly cracked black pepper
5 tbsp pomegranate seeds
4 tbsp roughly chopped fresh parsley

Combine the lemon juice, olive oil, ginger, coriander, and garlic in a medium bowl and mix well. Sprinkle the squab generously with salt and pepper, and arrange them in a single layer in a shallow glass baking dish. Pour the marinade over the birds, turning to coat on all sides. Cover with cling film and refrigerate for at least 1 and up to 3 hours.

Cook the bacon over a medium heat in a sauté pan until crisp (6–8 minutes). Transfer to kitchen paper to drain.

Rub the figs with olive oil and sprinkle generously with salt and pepper.

Make the glaze: combine the honey, mint, ginger, lemon juice, and chilli flakes in a small bowl, and mix well.

Build a multilevel fire in your grill (see p31). When the coals are all ignited, the flames have died down, and the temperature is medium-hot (see p34), you're ready to cook.

Arrange the squab on the hot side of the grill and cook until just cooked through (5–7 minutes per side). To check for doneness, cut into the thickest part of one of the thighs; the juices should run clear, and there should be only a hint of pink near the bone. When the squab are done, move them to the cooler side of the grill. Brush generously with the glaze, and let sit for 2 minutes more on each side. (Be careful not to burn the glaze.)

When you move the squab, put the figs on the hot side of the grill, cut-side down. Cook until just browned (2–3 minutes). Arrange the squab and figs on a serving plate. Scatter over the bacon, pomegranate seeds, and parsley.

SMOKY CHICKEN THIGHS
WITH MAPLE BARBECUE SAUCE

We're big fans of chicken thighs because they're very tasty and easy to prepare, and they have just enough fat to stay moist on the grill. This is a deliciously sweet, sticky, old-school treatment most often used with wings, but we like it even better with thighs. These are not only great hot off the grill (*see overleaf*), but when they're cold, too, making them perfect for picnics.

Serves 4

THE CHICKEN

8 large chicken thighs, bone-in, about
    225g (8oz) each

THE SPICE RUB

2 tbsp ground coriander

2 tbsp paprika

2 tbsp ground cumin

2 tbsp soft dark brown sugar

2 tbsp freshly cracked black pepper

1 tbsp kosher salt

THE BARBECUE SAUCE

4 tbsp tomato ketchup
5 tbsp maple syrup
Juice of 1 lemon (about 4 tbsp)

Light a fire well over to one side of your grill, using enough coals to fill a large shoebox. When the fire has died down and the coals are covered with white ash, you're ready to cook.

Combine the spice rub ingredients in a small bowl and mix well.

Coat the thighs generously with the spice rub, pressing gently to be sure it adheres, then arrange them, skin-side down, on the side of the grill away from the coals, being careful that none of the meat is directly over the coals. Put the lid on the grill with the vents open one-quarter of the way and cook for about 1 hour, adding a handful of fresh charcoal and flipping the thighs over after 30 minutes. To check for doneness, cut into one of the thighs at its thickest point; there should be no redness near the bone.

While the chicken is on the grill, combine the ketchup, maple syrup, and lemon juice in a small bowl and mix well. Baste the chicken with the sauce during the last 10 minutes of cooking, and serve the remaining sauce along with the smoked thighs.

GLAZED PHEASANT BREASTS

When we were growing up, the *ne plus ultra* of fine dining was breast of pheasant "under glass". Unfortunately, that rather silly treatment gave a bad name to a perfectly good piece of fowl. We try to resurrect its reputation here by serving it with a take on the traditional Cumberland sauce, adapted for ease and grilling pleasure.

Serves 4–6

THE PHEASANT

6 boneless pheasant breasts, 140–175g (5–6oz) each
2 tbsp olive oil
Kosher salt and freshly cracked black pepper
3 tbsp roughly chopped fresh thyme leaves

THE GLAZE

120ml (4fl oz) port wine
85g (3oz) redcurrant jelly
1 tbsp finely chopped orange zest
Kosher salt and freshly cracked black pepper to taste

Build a fire in your grill. When the coals are all ignited, the flames have died down, and the temperature is medium (*see p34*), you're ready to cook.

Make the glaze: combine the port, redcurrant jelly, orange zest, and salt and pepper in a small saucepan and, on the hob, bring it to a simmer over a medium heat, whisking until the jelly melts. Adjust the heat so the glaze simmers gently and cook until it has reduced by half and has a sticky consistency (25–30 minutes). Transfer the glaze to a small bowl and set it aside.

Rub the pheasant breasts with the olive oil, sprinkle them generously with salt and pepper, and pat the thyme onto them. Put them on the grill directly over the coals and cook for 6–8 minutes per side, brushing with the glaze for the last 30 seconds of cooking. To check for doneness, poke the meat with your finger to test its firmness (*see p37*); if you're unsure, cut into one to be sure that there is just a hint of pink at the centre. Serve, passing the remaining glaze on the side.

DEVILLED GAME HENS
WITH CARAMELISED ONIONS, PANCETTA, AND SAGE

This is our modernized version of the approach that the great 19th-century French chef Auguste Escoffier used with grilled food, which involves lots of breadcrumbs. Today it's quite unusual, but it's still very delicious. And game hens are fun to serve because it seems indulgent – almost decadent – when each person gets a whole bird.

Serves 4

Onion, pancetta, and sage garnish

THE HENS

4 Rock Cornish hens, about 675g (1½lb) each (or substitute poussins, about 450g/1lb each), butterflied with backbone removed

Kosher salt and freshly cracked black pepper

THE BREADCRUMB COATING

5 tbsp wholegrain mustard

1 tbsp Worcestershire sauce

1 tbsp Tabasco

60g (2oz) fresh breadcrumbs

2 tbsp roughly chopped fresh parsley

1 tbsp finely chopped fresh garlic

Kosher salt and freshly cracked black pepper to taste

THE GARNISH

225g (8oz) pancetta, diced small (or substitute bacon)

2 red onions, peeled and sliced thin

Kosher salt and freshly cracked black pepper to taste

1 tbsp roughly chopped fresh sage

Build a multilevel fire in your grill (*see p31*). When the coals are all ignited, the fire has died down, and the temperature is medium (*see p34*), you're ready to cook.

Sprinkle the hens generously with salt and pepper, place them skin-side down on the hotter side of the grill, and cook until the skin is nicely browned (about 15 minutes). (If the hens start to darken too quickly, move them to the cooler side of the grill for the remainder of the 15 minutes.) Flip the hens over and cook until the other side is also brown and crisp (about 15 minutes more). (You may have to decrease the cooking time slightly if you are using poussins.) To check for doneness, cut into one of the thighs, or where the wing meets the breast: the meat should be opaque throughout, with no pink near the bone.

While the hens are on the grill, cook the pancetta on the hob in a large sauté pan over a medium-low heat, stirring frequently, until it is crisp and brown (about 7 minutes). Transfer the pancetta to kitchen paper to drain, and discard all but 2 tbsp of the rendered fat in the pan. Add the onions to the pan, season with salt and pepper, and sauté, stirring occasionally, until they are well-caramelised (20–30 minutes). Add the sage during the last minute or two of cooking. Remove the pan from the heat.

Combine the mustard, Worcestershire sauce, and Tabasco in a small bowl and mix well. In another bowl, combine the breadcrumbs, parsley, garlic, and salt and pepper and toss until evenly mixed.

When the hens are just done, move them to the cooler side of the grill, slather them with the mustard mixture, and sprinkle them generously with the breadcrumbs, pressing gently to be sure they adhere. Leave the hens on the grill for another minute or two to toast the crumbs, then transfer them to a serving plate. Top each with some of the caramelised onions, sprinkle with the reserved pancetta, and serve.

Breadcrumb coating

SPICY GRILLED CHICKEN WINGS

Among the many virtues of chicken wings, perhaps the best of all is the very high ratio of crisp, super-flavourful skin to meat. To take advantage of this, we toss the wings with a spicy herb mixture right after they come off the grill, so the skin gets nicely coated. You probably already know this, but these make an excellent snack to serve when you have friends over to watch the big match.

Serves 4

THE WINGS

1.35kg (3lb) chicken wings

3 tbsp olive oil

2 tbsp smoked paprika *picante* (hot) (preferably the Spanish *pimentón de La Vera*)

Kosher salt and freshly cracked black pepper

THE DRESSING

4 tbsp extra virgin olive oil

Juice of 1 lemon (about 4 tbsp)

4 tbsp roughly chopped fresh herbs: any combination of parsley, sage, rosemary, thyme, and oregano

2 tbsp dry sherry

1 tbsp finely chopped fresh garlic

1 tbsp chilli pepper flakes

Kosher salt and freshly cracked black pepper to taste

Build a fire in your grill. When the coals are all ignited, the flames have died down, and the temperature is medium (*see p34*), you're ready to cook.

Cut each wing into 3 sections. Discard the wing tips or save them for stock.

Rub the wing pieces with oil, sprinkle them with smoked paprika, salt, and pepper, then put them on the grill directly over the coals and cook, turning occasionally, until they are golden-brown (10–15 minutes). To check for doneness, cut into one to make sure there is no redness near the bone.

While the wings are on the grill, combine the olive oil, lemon juice, fresh herbs, sherry, garlic, chilli flakes, and salt and pepper in a bowl large enough to hold all of the wings; mix well.

As the wings come off the grill, add them to the bowl, turning to coat with the dressing. Serve the wings hot, right out of the bowl, with plenty of paper napkins.

PUT A LID ON IT

THERE'S NOTHING WE LIKE BETTER THAN RELAXING WITH FRIENDS, HAVING A COUPLE OF COLD BEERS, WHILE SOMETHING DELICIOUS IS QUIETLY SOAKING UP THE SMOKY FLAVOURS OF THE FIRE. IT'S THE EPITOME OF OUR FAVOURITE FOOD MANTRA: ''WORK SMARTER, NOT HARDER''. EVEN BETTER — THE RESULTS ARE FANTASTIC.

TEXAN SLOW-COOKED BEEF
WITH BARBECUE SAUCE

In Texas, beef brisket is the barbecue cut of choice. It is perhaps the ultimate example of taking a tough, gnarly piece of meat and transforming it into a super-tender delicacy through long, slow cooking. As with the slow-cooked pork barbecue of North Carolina (*see pp196–9*), the preferred method is to make a night of it, putting the brisket on in the early evening and letting it cook until daylight. But this also makes a very good pastime for a lazy Saturday, a great way to spend time hanging out with friends then ending the day with a spectacularly delicious meal. The sauce, which has a little kick to it, can be made up to a week in advance, and then kept covered and refrigerated.

Serves 8 to 10

THE MEAT

1 beef brisket, 4.5–5.5kg (10–12lb)
3 tbsp olive oil
4 tbsp kosher salt
4 tbsp freshly cracked black pepper

THE SAUCE

150ml (5fl oz) tomato ketchup
120ml (4fl oz) cider vinegar
4 tbsp soft dark brown sugar
2 tbsp hot sauce of your choice
1 tsp ground cumin
1 tsp paprika
1 tsp kosher salt
1 tsp freshly cracked black pepper

Light a fire well over to one side of your grill, using enough coals to fill a large shoebox.

Rub the brisket with the oil and coat it evenly with salt and pepper, pressing gently to make sure it adheres.

When the fire has died down and the coals are covered with white ash, place the brisket on the side of the grill away from the coals, being careful that none of the meat is directly over the coals. Put the lid on the grill with the vents open one-quarter of the way and cook, adding a handful of fresh charcoal every 30 minutes or so, for 8–10 hours. To test for doneness, stick a big fork in the meat and try to lift it up – if it falls off the fork, it's done.

While the beef is on the grill, make the sauce: combine the sauce ingredients in a small saucepan and mix well. On the hob over a medium heat, bring the mixture to a simmer and cook for 5 minutes to blend the flavours, then remove from the heat and transfer to a serving bowl.

To serve, slice the brisket thinly across the grain, and pass the barbecue sauce on the side.

SUPER-HOT JERK PORK SHOULDER
WITH SPICED PINEAPPLE CHUTNEY

Over the past few years, jerk has become one of the most widely interpreted (and misinterpreted) cooking methods in the world. This pork shoulder, which we accompany with a spicy chutney that also features the flavours of Jamaica, may not be fully authentic, but it's pretty close. Note that the meat may need up to 8 hours to cook.

Serves 8

THE MEAT

1 boneless pork shoulder roast, about 2.25kg (5lb)
Kosher salt and freshly cracked black pepper

THE CHUTNEY

2 tbsp olive oil
½ red onion, peeled and diced medium
½ red pepper, cored, deseeded, and diced medium
1 small or ½ large ripe pineapple, peeled and cut into 1cm (½in) chunks
2 tbsp good-quality curry powder
1 tbsp peeled and finely chopped fresh ginger
Pinch of allspice
5 tbsp cider vinegar
2 tbsp soft dark brown sugar
Kosher salt and freshly cracked black pepper to taste

THE JERK SEASONING

4 tbsp American yellow mustard
4 tbsp red wine vinegar
4 tbsp roughly chopped spring onions, including green tops
3 habanero or Scotch Bonnet chilli peppers, chopped, including seeds and ribs
3 garlic cloves, peeled
3 tbsp dried thyme
2 tbsp dried oregano
2 tbsp treacle

Spiced pineapple chutney

Light a fire well over to one side of your grill, using enough coals to fill half a shoebox. When the fire has died down and the coals are covered in white ash, then you're ready to cook.

Meanwhile, make the jerk seasoning: combine the ingredients in a blender or food processor and purée.

Dry the pork with kitchen paper, season generously with salt and pepper, and rub it all over with the jerk seasoning.

Place the pork roast on the side of the grill away from the coals, being careful that none of the meat is directly over the coals. Put the lid on the grill with the vents open one-quarter of the way and cook, adding a handful of fresh charcoal about every 30 minutes, until the pork is done (5–8 hours). To check for doneness, plunge a big fork straight down into the meat and try to lift it up off the grill – if the fork slides out easily, the meat is done; if the meat hangs on to the fork, give it more time.

While the pork is roasting, make the pineapple chutney: on the hob, heat the oil in a large sauté pan over a medium-high heat until hot but not smoking. Add the onion and red pepper and sauté, stirring occasionally, until the onion is transparent (7–9 minutes). Stir in the pineapple, curry powder, ginger, and allspice and sauté, stirring occasionally, for about 3 minutes more. Add the vinegar and brown sugar, bring to the boil, lower the heat and simmer gently for 6–8 minutes, stirring occasionally to keep the mixture from sticking to the pan. When the chutney has thickened, remove the pan from the heat, season to taste with salt and pepper, and transfer to a serving dish. (The chutney can be made up to 5 days in advance, covered and refrigerated.)

When the pork is done, remove it from the grill and allow it to cool slightly. When it is cool enough to handle, slice the meat and serve it with the pineapple chutney.

FLAVOUR FOOTPRINT WEST INDIES-CARIBBEAN

The flavours of the West Indies reflect the region's complex history. Allspice and Scotch Bonnet peppers, for example, originated in the islands, while bananas and coconuts were brought by Europeans, and the widely popular curry powder arrived with Indian indentured servants who were brought in to work the plantations after slavery had ended. From this melting pot of ingredients has come a group of distinctive, boldly flavoured cuisines. Just try a couple of the dishes here, and you'll bring the ease and excitement of the islands right into your kitchen.

Red Onion-Tamarind Chutney
Makes about 450g (1lb)

The unique earthy-tart flavour of tamarind gives this chutney its distinctive taste. We like it with a big, juicy pork roast, although it's also good with beef and lamb.

2 tbsp olive oil
2 large red onions, peeled and sliced
1 tbsp peeled and finely chopped fresh ginger
2 tbsp tamarind paste
1 tbsp good-quality curry powder
75ml (2½fl oz) cider vinegar
5 tbsp soft dark brown sugar
Kosher salt and freshly cracked black pepper to taste
3 tbsp roughly chopped fresh mint

Heat the oil in a large sauté pan over a medium-high heat until hot but not smoking. Add the onions and sauté, stirring occasionally, until they are golden-brown (11–13 minutes). Add the ginger, tamarind, and curry powder, and sauté, stirring frequently, until fragrant (about 2 minutes more). Add the brown sugar and vinegar and bring to a simmer, stirring to dissolve the sugar. Reduce the heat to low and simmer gently, stirring frequently to prevent scorching, until the chutney thickens (about 10 minutes). Season with salt and pepper, remove from the heat, and stir in the mint. This chutney will keep, covered and refrigerated, for up to 10 days.

West Indian-Style Steak Relish
Makes about 180g (6oz)

We may call it "steak relish" — and it is totally awesome served with a grilled steak — but this is also great with chops.

75g (2½oz) tamarind pulp
1 tbsp mustard powder
1 tbsp finely chopped fresh garlic
1 tbsp peeled and finely chopped fresh ginger
1 tbsp finely chopped fresh chilli pepper of your choice
1 tbsp treacle or molasses
Kosher salt and freshly cracked black pepper to taste

Place the tamarind pulp in a bowl with enough hot water to cover and let it stand for 30 minutes to soften. Mix the tamarind with all the remaining ingredients and stir well. This relish will keep, covered and refrigerated, for 3–4 days.

West Indian-Style
Steak Relish

Guava Barbecue Sauce
Makes about 500ml (16fl oz)

You'll love this one with any kind of meat, fowl, or fish – either brush some on just for the last 30 seconds of grilling time, or serve as an accompaniment, or both.

240ml (8fl oz) tomato ketchup
5 tbsp guava juice (or substitute peach juice)
4 tbsp treacle or molasses
Juice of 2 limes (about 4 tbsp)
2 tbsp peeled and finely chopped fresh ginger
Kosher salt and freshly cracked black pepper to taste

Combine all the ingredients in a medium bowl and mix well. This sauce will keep, covered and refrigerated, for up to a week.

Pineapple-Curry Relish
Makes about 500g (1lb 2oz)

Although we particularly like it with grilled fish or chicken, this is an all-purpose relish that goes with almost anything.

450g (1lb) fresh pineapple, diced small
Juice of 2 limes (about 4 tbsp)
2 tbsp roughly chopped spring onions, green and white parts
1 tbsp finely chopped fresh chilli pepper of your choice
1 tbsp peeled and finely chopped fresh ginger
1 tbsp curry powder

Combine all the ingredients in a medium bowl and mix well. This relish will keep, covered and refrigerated, for 3–4 days.

SIGNATURE INGREDIENTS/TOP ROW (LEFT TO RIGHT) Tamarind, limes, nutmeg; **SECOND ROW** Ginger, guavas, orange; **THIRD ROW** Coconut, allspice, garlic; **BOTTOM ROW** Curry powder, chilli peppers, oregano.

Adobo Paste
Makes about 200g (7oz)

This works either as a last-minute rub before chicken, pork, or beef go on the grill, or a quick marinade (up to 4 hours).

4 tbsp paprika (not smoked)
3 tbsp dried oregano
2 tbsp finely chopped fresh garlic
1 tbsp ground cumin
1 tbsp chilli pepper flakes
1 tbsp finely chopped lime zest
2 tbsp olive oil
Kosher salt and freshly cracked black pepper to taste

Combine all the ingredients in a small bowl and mix well. This paste will keep, covered and refrigerated, for 2–3 days.

Pineapple-Curry Relish

HERB-CRUSTED PORK LOIN
WITH MOSTARDA DI FRUTTA

Pork, fruit, and mustard are one of those trios that just seem right. So we put together a herb-rubbed pork loin with our version of Italian *mostarda di frutta*, a tasty mix of preserved fruits flavoured with mustard seeds – using mustard powder and dried fruit to make it easier. You can use a boneless pork loin, but the meat on a bone-in one has richer, deeper flavour.

Serves 6–8

THE MEAT

4 tbsp olive oil
4 tbsp roughly chopped fresh sage
2 tbsp crushed fennel seeds
2 tbsp finely chopped fresh garlic
1 centre-cut loin of pork, bone-in, about 2.25kg (5lb)
Kosher salt and freshly cracked black pepper to taste

THE MOSTARDA

240ml (8fl oz) water
45g (1½oz) mustard powder
120ml (4fl oz) distilled white vinegar
4 tbsp soft dark brown sugar
1 tbsp peeled and finely chopped fresh ginger
60g (2oz) raisins
280g (10oz) combination of diced fruit: dried apricots, dried peaches, dried figs, and dried mango

Kosher salt and freshly cracked black pepper to taste

Light a fire well over to one side of your grill, using enough coals to fill half a shoebox.

Mash together the oil, sage, fennel seeds, and garlic in a small bowl to form a loose paste. Dry the pork well with kitchen paper, season it generously with salt and pepper, and rub the pork all over with the seasoning paste.

When the fire has died down and the coals are covered in white ash, place the roast on the side of the grill away from the coals, being careful that none of the meat is directly over the coals. Put the lid on the grill with the vents open one-quarter of the way and cook, adding a handful of fresh charcoal about every 30 minutes, until the pork is done (about 1 hour). To check for doneness, insert a meat thermometer into the centre of the roast, without touching the bone; let it sit for 5 seconds, then read the temperature: 57°C (134°F) for medium, 66°C (150°F) for medium-well done, and 71°C (160°F) for well-done. We like to pull the meat at 64°C (147°F). When the roast is done to your liking, remove it from the grill, cover it loosely with foil, and let it rest for about 20 minutes.

While the pork cooks, make the *mostarda*: whisk the water and mustard powder together in a small bowl until smooth; set aside. On the hob, combine the vinegar, brown sugar, and ginger in a small saucepan over a medium-high heat, stirring until the sugar dissolves and the mixture comes to the boil. Reduce the heat to low and simmer, stirring often, until thickened (about 10 minutes). Add the mustard and mix well, then stir in all of the dried fruits and continue to simmer gently until thickened (15–20 minutes more). Add salt and pepper to taste, and transfer to a serving bowl.

To serve, carve the pork from the bone, arrange the meat on a serving plate, and pass the *mostarda* on the side.

SIMPLE SMOKE-ROASTED WHOLE CHICKEN

This is a classic: chickens flavoured with garlic and rosemary and cooked with the indirect heat and smoke of a slow, low fire. It's the kind of dish you could serve once a week all summer long and not get tired of. And, if you're not familiar with the technique of smoke-roasting (*see also p18*), this is a great dish to start with. It's simple and direct, but ends up with great, smoky flavour.

Serves 6

THE INGREDIENTS

2 whole chickens, 1.35kg (3lb) each
3 tbsp olive oil
3 tbsp finely chopped fresh garlic
3 tbsp roughly chopped fresh rosemary
2 tbsp kosher salt
2 tbsp freshly cracked black pepper
2 lemons, halved

Light a fire well over to one side of your grill, using enough coals to fill 1½ large shoeboxes.

Place one chicken on your work surface, breast side up, and push down hard to flatten it as much as possible. Repeat with the second bird, then rub both all over with the olive oil. Mash together the garlic, rosemary, salt, and pepper, and coat the chickens evenly with this herb mixture, pressing gently to be sure it adheres.

When the fire has died down and the coals are covered with white ash, place the chickens on the side of the grill away from the coals, breast side down, legs facing toward the coals, being careful that none of the meat is directly over the coals. Put the lid on the grill with the vents open one-quarter of the way. Cook for 30 minutes, then turn the chickens breast side up, add another ½ shoebox full of fresh charcoal, and continue cooking for 30–45 minutes more. To check for doneness, make a cut into the thickest part of one thigh, all the way to the bone; there should be no sign of pink. It's not easy to take the temperature of a flattened bird, but if you do use a thermometer, look for a final temperature of 71°C (160°F).

When the chickens are done, transfer them to a cutting board, cover loosely with foil, and allow them to rest for about 10 minutes. Carve each chicken into 6 pieces, squeeze the lemon halves over them, and serve.

SMOKE-ROASTED BARBECUE CHICKEN

This is a slightly more complex approach to grilling a whole chicken than the plain-and-simple version on p191, but it's still pretty much a breeze to make. Since the birds are never directly over the coals there's no need to worry about burning sugars, so we can coat them with a simple but luscious ketchup-brown sugar paste before they go onto the grill. We then serve them with a thick, gooey sauce in the traditional barbecue manner.

Serves 6

THE CHICKEN

180ml (6fl oz) tomato ketchup
2 tbsp soft dark brown sugar
1 tsp ground coriander
1 tsp ground cumin
2 whole chickens, 1.35kg (3lb) each
Kosher salt and freshly cracked black pepper

THE SAUCE

240ml (8fl oz) apple juice
120ml (4fl oz) cider vinegar
2 tbsp finely chopped orange zest
2 tbsp soft dark brown sugar
1 tablespoon celery seed

Light a fire well over to one side of your grill, using enough coals to fill 1½ large shoeboxes.

Combine the ketchup, brown sugar, coriander, and cumin in a small bowl and mix well.

Place one chicken on a work surface, breast-side up, and push down hard to flatten it as much as possible. Repeat with the second bird. Sprinkle them generously with salt and pepper and coat thoroughly with the ketchup mixture.

When the fire has died down and the coals are covered with white ash, place the chickens on the side of the grill away from the coals, breast-side down, legs facing toward the coals, being careful that none of the meat is directly over the coals. Put the lid on the grill with the vents open one-quarter of the way. Cook for 30 minutes, then turn the chickens breast-side up, add another ½ shoebox of fresh charcoal, and continue cooking for 30–45 minutes more. To check for doneness, make a cut into the thickest part of one thigh, all the way to the bone; there should be no sign of pink. It's not easy to take the temperature of a flattened bird, but if you do use a thermometer, look for a final temperature of 71°C (160°F).

Meanwhile, make the barbecue sauce on the hob: combine the sauce ingredients in a small saucepan over a medium-high heat and bring just to the boil. Reduce the heat to low and simmer, stirring frequently, until thick, syrupy, and reduced by about two-thirds (about 20 minutes). Transfer the sauce to a serving bowl.

When the chickens are done, transfer them to a cutting board, cover loosely with foil, and allow them to rest for about 10 minutes. Carve each chicken into 6 pieces and serve, along with the barbecue sauce.

SMOKE-ROASTED BEEF WITH GREEN PEPPERCORN SAUCE

This is a pretty straightforward roast beef with traditional green peppercorn sauce — except, of course, that the beef is coated with a layer of black peppercorns, and roasting it on the grill gives it a lovely deep, smoky flavour that's the perfect complement to the beef's full-on taste. The decadent sauce makes this a great dish for special occasions.

Serves 10–12

THE MEAT

1 beef topside joint, 2.7–3.6kg (6–8lb)
3 tbsp olive oil
115g (4oz) freshly cracked black pepper
115g (4oz) kosher salt

THE SAUCE

240ml (8fl oz) brandy
45g (1¼oz) green peppercorns, drained and rinsed
480ml (16fl oz) beef stock
240ml (8fl oz) double cream
115g (4oz) unsalted butter, diced and kept cold
4 tbsp roughly chopped fresh parsley
Kosher salt and freshly cracked black pepper to taste

Light a fire well over to one side of your grill, using enough coals to fill a large shoebox.

Rub the beef with the oil and coat it evenly with the pepper and salt, pressing gently to make sure it adheres.

When the fire has died down and the coals are covered with white ash, place the beef on the side of the grill away from the coals, being careful that none of the meat is directly over the coals. Put the lid on the grill with the vents open one-quarter of the way and cook, adding a handful of fresh charcoal every 30 minutes or so, until the beef is done to your liking (45 minutes to 1 hour for medium-rare). To check for doneness, poke the roast with your finger to test its firmness (*see p37*). If you're unsure, insert a meat thermometer in the centre of the roast and let it sit for 5 seconds, then read the temperature: you're looking for 49°C (120°F) for rare, 52°C (126°F) for medium-rare, 57°C (134°F) for medium, 65°C (150°F) for medium-well, and 71°C (160°F) for well done. (We like to pull the roast at 50°C/122°F.) When the roast is done, remove it from the grill, cover it loosely with foil, and allow it to rest for at least 15 minutes before carving.

While the beef is cooking, make the sauce on the hob: combine the brandy and green peppercorns in a medium sauté pan over a medium-high heat. Bring to the boil, adjust the heat to medium, and simmer until the brandy is syrupy (about 3 minutes). Add the beef stock and continue to simmer until reduced by one-third (about 15 minutes more). Stir in the cream and simmer until slightly thickened (about 10 minutes more). Turn the heat to low, then gradually whisk in the cold butter, a few chunks at a time. When all the butter has been added, remove the sauce from the heat and stir in the parsley and salt and pepper.

To serve, cut the beef into slices, arrange them on a serving plate, and run a ribbon of sauce down the middle of the slices. Pass the remaining sauce on the side.

SOUTHERN SLOW-COOKED PORK
WITH COLE SLAW

This is the traditional North Carolina pork barbecue that I (Chris) grew up with. To my mind, there is really no better food than this smoky, fall-apart-tender pork. If you really want to do it right, you should start it at about midnight and stay up all night, drinking beers and telling stories around the fire as the pork cooks. Whenever you cook it, though, it's the perfect meal for large gatherings. It also freezes very well, so don't be afraid of leftovers.

Serves 15

THE MEAT

2 boneless pork roasts,
    1.8–2.25kg (4–5lb) each
3 tbsp olive oil

THE RUB

4 tbsp paprika
2 tbsp kosher salt
2 tbsp freshly cracked black pepper
2 tbsp ground cumin
2 tbsp chilli powder
2 tbsp soft dark brown sugar
1 tablespoon cayenne pepper

THE COLE SLAW

350g (12oz) mayonnaise
5 tbsp distilled white vinegar
5 tbsp granulated sugar
1 tbsp celery seeds
1 head green cabbage, finely shredded
2 carrots, finely grated
Kosher salt and freshly cracked black pepper to taste

THE SAUCE

240ml (8fl oz) distilled white vinegar
240ml (8fl oz) cider vinegar
1 tbsp granulated sugar
1 tbsp chilli pepper flakes
1 tbsp Tabasco
Kosher salt and freshly cracked black pepper to taste

THE EXTRAS

White fluffy sandwich bread or hamburger buns

Light a fire well over to one side of your grill, using enough coals to fill a large shoebox.

Combine the spice rub ingredients in a small bowl and mix well. Rub the pork roasts with the oil and coat them generously with the spice rub, pressing gently to make sure it adheres.

When the fire has died down and the coals are covered with white ash, place the pork on the side of the grill away from the coals, being careful that none of the meat is directly over the coals. Put the lid on the grill with the vents open one-quarter of the way, and cook, adding a handful of fresh charcoal every 30 minutes or so, for 7–9 hours. To test for doneness, stick a big fork in the meat and try to lift it up – if it falls off the fork, it's done.

Meanwhile, make the cole slaw: combine the mayonnaise, vinegar, sugar, and celery seeds in a large bowl and mix well. Add the cabbage and carrots and toss well to blend. Season with salt and pepper, cover, and refrigerate until serving time.

Now make the barbecue sauce: combine the vinegars, sugar, chilli flakes, Tabasco, and salt and pepper in a medium bowl and mix well.

Chop or shred the pork (if it's still too hot to handle, use two forks to pull it apart) and mix it with as much of the sauce as you like. Pile it onto the bread or buns, top with the cole slaw, and serve.

SMOKE-ROASTED WHOLE DUCK
WITH ORANGE, GINGER, AND HOISIN-CHILLI SAUCE

A whole smoked duck is a beautiful thing to behold – and it's awesomely delicious, too. It's also pretty simple, although you have to remember to start it the day before you want to serve it, since it needs to sit in the refrigerator overnight to absorb the flavours of the sesame, ginger, and orange. The sauce is easy too, but if you're feeling lazy you can just swab the finished duck with a little hoisin sauce.

Serves 2

THE DUCK

1 whole duck, 1.8–2.25kg (4–5lb)
1 tbsp sesame oil
3 tbsp freshly cracked white pepper
2 tbsp peeled and finely chopped fresh ginger
2 tbsp finely chopped orange zest
2 tbsp kosher salt

THE SAUCE

5 tbsp hoisin sauce
3 tbsp roughly chopped fresh coriander
2 tbsp chilli-garlic sauce
1 tbsp peeled and finely chopped fresh ginger

Use a fork to prick a dozen or so holes through the duck skin in the area between the wing and the breast, making sure you get down to the layer of fat, but being careful not to puncture the meat underneath. Pat the duck dry with paper towels, then rub it all over with the sesame oil.

Combine the white pepper, ginger, orange zest, and salt in a small bowl and mash together; rub this mixture all over the surface of the duck. Put the duck on a plate and refrigerate it overnight, uncovered.

Light a fire well over to one side of your grill, using about enough coals to fill 2 shoeboxes.

Remove the duck from the refrigerator and gently pat it dry again. When the fire has died down and the coals are covered with white ash, put the duck on the side of the grill away from the coals, with the legs closest to the coals. Be careful that none of the duck is directly over the coals. Put the lid on the grill with the vents one-quarter of the way open and cook, adding a ½ shoebox full of fresh charcoal after the first 30 minutes of cooking. About 10 minutes later (after 40 minutes of cooking), reposition the duck so that the breast is closer to the fire. Cook for about another 30–50 minutes. To check for doneness, pierce one of the legs and make sure that the juices run clear; as a second test, twist the leg gently – the joint should feel slightly loose in its socket.

While the duck is roasting, make the sauce: combine the hoisin, coriander, chilli-garlic sauce, and ginger in a small bowl and mix well.

When the duck is ready, transfer it to a cutting board. To carve, slice straight down to one side of the breastbone, following the shape of the carcass. Repeat on the other side of the breastbone. Cut through the wing joints, and put each duck half on a plate. Top each serving with a drizzle of sauce, and pass the remaining sauce on the side.

CUBAN SMOKED PORK
WITH CORIANDER VINAIGRETTE

Southerners aren't the only ones who know how to smoke-roast a mean hunk of pork (*see pp196–9*). Cuban cooks are experts in this field, too, so here we add some island flavours to the super-tender, fall-apart smoky meat. We particularly like this served with warm tortillas to wrap around the tendrils of meat.

Serves 8–10

THE MEAT

4 tbsp finely chopped fresh garlic

4 tbsp freshly cracked coriander seeds (or substitute 2 tbsp ground coriander)

4 tbsp paprika

3 tbsp kosher salt

3 tbsp freshly cracked black pepper

1 boneless pork shoulder roast, about 2.7kg (6lb)

4 tbsp olive oil

THE VINAIGRETTE

5 tbsp extra virgin olive oil

5 tbsp red wine vinegar

4 tbsp roughly chopped fresh cilantro

2 tbsp hot sauce of your choice

1 tsp finely chopped fresh garlic

Kosher salt and freshly cracked black pepper to taste

Light a fire well over to one side of your grill, using enough coals to fill a shoebox.

Combine the garlic, coriander, paprika, salt, and pepper in a small bowl and mix well. Rub the pork with the oil and coat it generously with the spice mixture, pressing gently to be sure it adheres.

When the fire has died down and the coals are covered with white ash, place the pork on the side of the grill away from the coals, being careful that none of the meat is directly over the coals. Put the lid on the grill with the vents open one-quarter of the way and cook, adding a handful of fresh charcoal every 30 minutes or so, for 5–8 hours. To test for doneness, stick a big fork in the roast and try to lift it up – if it falls off the fork, it's done.

Meanwhile, make the vinaigrette: combine the olive oil, vinegar, coriander, hot sauce, garlic, salt, and pepper in a small bowl and whisk to combine thoroughly.

Chop or shred the pork, drizzle it with the vinaigrette, and serve, either by itself or with burger buns or tortillas.

ORANGE AND BOURBON-BRINED WHOLE TURKEY

Here's a Southern-style turkey that's great not just for the festive season, but any time you have a crowd coming over. Brining helps keep the bird moist during the rather rigorous smoking process, so what you end up with is tender meat imbued with a wonderful smoky flavour. (If you want to avoid taking up most of your refrigerator, you can brine the turkey in a large cooler with ice packs floating in it, so long as you change the ice packs frequently.) Good as this is served warm from the grill, it's even better for sandwiches the next day.

Serves 6

THE BRINE

4 litres (7 pints) water
2 cups kosher salt
350g (12oz) granulated sugar
240ml (8fl oz) bourbon whiskey
2 oranges, sliced

THE TURKEY

5.5–6.5kg (12–15lb) turkey, giblets removed
Freshly cracked black pepper to taste
2 apples (variety of your choice), cored and quartered
1 red onion, peeled and quartered
3 tbsp roughly chopped fresh sage

Combine the brine ingredients in a large container that the turkey will easily fit into, and stir to dissolve the salt and sugar. Rinse the turkey well inside and out, then place it in the container, making sure it is completely submerged in the brine. Refrigerate for 24–48 hours, turning every 12 hours.

Light a fire well over to one side of your grill, using enough coals to fill a large shoebox. When the fire has died down and the coals are covered with white ash, remove the turkey from the brine and rinse it well, inside and out. Dry the bird with kitchen paper, sprinkle the cavity generously with pepper, and stuff it with the apples, onion, and sage.

Place the turkey on the side of the grill away from the coals, being careful that none of the bird is directly over the coals. Put the lid on the grill with the vents open one-quarter of the way and cook, adding a handful of fresh charcoal about every 30 minutes, until the juices run clear when you pierce the thigh with a fork (2½–3 hours). Turn the turkey around at least twice during this time, or more often if the side nearest the heat seems to be cooking too quickly. (To double-check doneness with a meat thermometer, insert it in the pit between the breast and leg; when the thermometer reads 71°C (160°F), the bird is done.)

Remove the bird from the grill, cover it loosely with foil, and allow it to rest for at least 15 minutes. Discard the apples and onions and carve it up.

GLAZED ROAST LEG OF PORK WITH HONEY MUSTARD SAUCE

This is perfect when you're having a group of people over: delicious, easy to prepare, and unusual enough to cause a bit of comment. If you have the time and inclination to brine it in advance, it will be more tender and flavourful, but it is delicious without brining, too.

Serves 10–12

THE MEAT

1 pork leg, bone-in with rind on, 3.5–4.5kg (8–10lb)
360ml (12fl oz) freshly squeezed orange juice
360ml (12fl oz) pineapple juice
3 tbsp roughly chopped fresh sage
25 whole cloves
5 tbsp wholegrain mustard
5 tbsp honey

THE BRINE (OPTIONAL)

3 litres (5¼ pints) water
480ml (16fl oz) dark rum
225g (8oz) soft dark brown sugar
225g (8oz) kosher salt
2 tbsp ground allspice

Score diagonal cuts both ways into the rind of the pork with a sharp knife to make a diamond pattern all over it.

If brining the pork, combine the brine ingredients in a container large enough to easily hold the pork and stir to dissolve the salt and sugar. Place the pork in the container, making sure that there is enough liquid to cover it completely. Refrigerate for at least 24 hours and up to 3 days, turning the pork over every 12 hours.

Combine the fruit juices in a small saucepan on the hob over a medium-high heat and bring to the boil. Lower the heat to a simmer and stir frequently, until the mixture is syrupy (about 25 minutes). Stir in the sage and set aside.

Light a fire well over to one side of your grill, using enough coals to fill a large shoebox. Remove the pork from the brine and dry it well with kitchen paper. (If you did not brine the pork, season it generously with kosher salt and black pepper.) Insert the cloves evenly across the rind in the points of the diamond-shaped cuts.

When the fire has died down and the coals are covered with white ash, place the pork on the side of the grill away from the coals, being careful that none of the meat is directly over the coals. Put the lid on the grill with the vents open one-quarter of the way, and cook, adding a handful of fresh charcoal every 30 minutes or so. Start checking for doneness after 2 hours; it may take up to 3 hours to fully cook. Baste it generously with the fruit juice glaze during the last 30 minutes of cooking. To check for doneness, insert a meat thermometer into the centre of the pork and let it sit for 5 seconds, then read the temperature: look for 57°C (134°F) for medium, 66°C (150°F) for medium-well, and 71°C (160°F) for well done; we pull the pork at 64°C (147°F). When the pork is done to your liking, remove it from the grill, cover it loosely with foil, and allow it to rest for 20–30 minutes before carving.

While the pork is resting, combine the mustard and honey in a small bowl and mix well. To serve, carve the pork into thick slices and pass the sauce on the side.

HERB-ROAST LEG OF LAMB WITH SWEET AND HOT APRICOTS

Lamb has enough intrinsic flavour to match not only the smokiness that is imparted by a smouldering fire, but also bold spice mixtures, like the lemony oregano paste we use here. And ever since we tasted it on the Greek island of Ikaria, we have loved the combination of lamb and apricots, although this spicy relish is equally delicious with chicken and pork.

Serves 6–8

THE MEAT

4 tbsp olive oil

4 tbsp roughly chopped fresh oregano (or you can use marjoram)

3 tbsp finely chopped garlic

2 tbsp finely chopped lemon zest

2 tbsp fennel seeds

1 leg of lamb, bone-in, 2.7–3.6kg (6–8lb), trimmed of all but 5mm (¼in) surface fat

Kosher salt and freshly cracked black pepper

THE APRICOTS

2 tbsp olive oil

1 medium red onion, peeled and diced small

1 tbsp peeled and finely chopped fresh ginger

2 tsp chilli pepper flakes

1 tbsp ground coriander

175g (6oz) dried apricots, cut into thin strips

120ml (4fl oz) red wine vinegar

2 tbsp soft dark brown sugar

Kosher salt and freshly cracked black pepper to taste

Light a fire well over to one side of your grill, using enough coals to fill half a shoebox.

Mash together the oil, oregano, garlic, lemon zest, and fennel seeds in a small bowl to make a loose paste. Dry the lamb with kitchen paper and sprinkle generously with salt and pepper. With the point of a paring knife, cut 8–10 slits, 5cm (2in) deep, into the meat, and push some of the herb paste into each. Rub any remaining paste over the surface.

When the flames have died down and the coals are covered in white ash, place the lamb on the side of the grill away from the coals, being careful that none of the meat is directly over the coals. Put the lid on with the vents open one-quarter of the way and cook, adding a handful of fresh charcoal about every 30 minutes, until the meat is done to your liking (1½–2 hours for medium-rare). To check for doneness, insert a meat thermometer into the thickest part (without touching the bone), let it sit for 5 seconds, then read it: you're looking for 49°C (120°F) for rare, 52°C (126°F) for medium-rare, 57°C (134°F) for medium, 65°C (150°F) for medium-well, and 71°C (160°F) for well done.

While the lamb is roasting, prepare the apricots: heat the oil in a large sauté pan on the hob over a medium-high heat until hot but not smoking. Add the onion and sauté, stirring occasionally, until transparent (7–9 minutes). Add the ginger, chilli pepper flakes, and coriander and stir until fragrant (about 1 minute). Add the apricots, vinegar, and brown sugar, and bring to the boil. Lower the heat and simmer gently until the apricots are tender (about 5 minutes). Remove from the heat, season with salt and pepper to taste, and transfer to a serving bowl.

When the lamb is done, remove it from the grill, cover loosely with foil, and let it rest for 10–15 minutes. Carve the lamb and serve it with the apricots on the side.

ON A STICK

WE LOVE SKEWERS FOR LOTS OF REASONS: STRINGING THEM TOGETHER SEEMS LIKE A GAME; MOST ARE AS EASY TO GRILL AS HOT DOGS; AND (MAYBE MOST IMPORTANTLY) YOU CAN GET AWAY WITH EATING THEM WITH YOUR FINGERS, SO THEY'RE GREAT PARTY FOOD. AND DID WE MENTION THAT THEY TASTE WONDERFUL?

THAI CHICKEN SATAY WITH MANGO-CHILLI SAUCE

On our last trip to Thailand, we were repeatedly reminded that the ambient level of heat in that cuisine is extreme. These tasty little sticks, fashioned out of chicken goujons, are pretty hot for our taste buds, but would seem relatively mild to even the least chilli-loving Thai. The barbecue sauce is also good with grilled fish or pork.

Serves 4 as an appetizer

THE SATAY

450g (1lb) chicken goujons, tendons removed
  (12–16 pieces)
2 tbsp chilli pepper flakes
1 tbsp good-quality curry powder
1 tbsp sesame oil
Kosher salt and freshly cracked black pepper to taste

THE SAUCE

120ml (4floz) tomato ketchup
120ml (4floz) mango juice
Juice of 2 limes (about 4 tbsp)
2 tbsp Thai fish sauce
  (or substitute soy sauce)
1–2 tbsp chilli-garlic paste,
  to taste
2 tbsp peeled and finely chopped fresh ginger
2 tbsp roughly chopped fresh Thai basil
  (or substitute Italian basil)
1 tbsp finely chopped fresh garlic

Build a fire in your grill. When the coals are all ignited, the flames have died down, and the temperature is medium-hot (*see p34*), you're ready to cook.

Combine the barbecue sauce ingredients in a bowl and mix well. Transfer about half the sauce to a small serving bowl and set aside.

Combine the chicken, chilli flakes, curry powder, oil, and salt and pepper in a bowl, and toss until evenly coated. Thread the chicken goujons onto skewers, put them on the grill directly over the coals, and cook until they are just done (3–4 minutes per side). Brush the chicken with the rest of the sauce during the last 30 seconds of cooking. To check for doneness, cut into one to make sure it is opaque all the way through.

Arrange the chicken satay on a serving plate with the small bowl of sauce for dipping, and serve immediately.

ISTANBUL: KEBAB PARADISE

Sprawling, mysterious, difficult, vigorously young but drenched in faded grandeur, Istanbul is one of the world's premier cities. It's also, as we found when we travelled there, the world capital of kebabs.

Oh, there may be other places in the Middle East or even Southeast Asia where grilled skewers are more pervasive, but in this continent-spanning city they are a class of food unto themselves. Each individual version has a specific history and provenance, so spending time there with our friend Ihsan, who grew up in the city, is a kind of culinary history lesson. One night, arriving after a long drive from Bodrum, in southeastern Turkey, we were startled when Ihsan swerved across traffic to stop at a particular kebab stand. "Cop sis!" he shouted, with his trademark excitement: "Garbage kebabs!" These southeast Anatolian specialities, he explained, used up all the little pieces of whatever was left over in restaurant kitchens at the end of the night – hence the name. And it was like that day after day, as we discovered an incredible profusion of kebab options – simple skewers of tiny livers sprinkled with salt and pepper; chunks of spicy *socuk* sausage alternating with *kasar* cheese; and infinite variations on the theme of lamb, either minced or in chunks, each with a different name depending on whether it is mixed with, for example, hot pepper paste and the spice mix known as *baharat*, or tomato paste and parsley – and on it went. There is more exotic food on the streets of this fascinating city (fatty, delicious intestine sandwiches, for example), but for sheer variety and inventiveness, the kebabs can't be beat. A plate of these, a glass of the curiously delicious salted yogurt drink called *ayran*, and you'll be happy as a pasha.

LAMB SHISH KEBABS
WITH MINTED YOGURT AND SCENTED PITTA BREAD

This is our tribute to the *kefta* and shish kebab served at Istanbul's Sultanahmet Keftah restaurant, possibly the best kebab shop in the world. If you can find the spice sumac, its lemony taste adds a distinctly Middle Eastern flavour to the warm pitta.

Serves 4

900g (2lb) boneless leg of lamb, cut into
  2.5cm (1in) cubes
2 red onions, peeled and cut into eighths
2 red peppers, cored, deseeded, and cut into eighths
4 tbsp olive oil
Kosher salt and freshly cracked black pepper to taste
Juice of 2 lemons (about 5 tbsp)
4 tbsp extra virgin olive oil
4 tbsp roughly chopped fresh oregano
1 tbsp finely chopped fresh garlic

For the yogurt:
350g (12oz) Greek-style yogurt
75g (2½oz) peeled, seeded, and diced
  cucumber
5 tbsp roughly chopped fresh mint
1 tsp ground white pepper
Kosher salt to taste

For the pitta bread:
4 pitta breads
2 tbsp olive oil
1 tbsp ground sumac (optional)

Build a fire in your grill. When the coals are all ignited, the flames have died down, and the temperature is medium-hot (*see p34*), you're ready to cook.

Combine the yogurt, cucumber, mint, and white pepper in a medium bowl and mix well. Season with salt to taste, cover, and refrigerate.

Combine the lamb, onions, peppers, oil, and salt and pepper in a large bowl and toss to coat. Thread the meat onto skewers, alternating with the peppers and onions. Put the skewers on the grill over the coals and cook until the vegetables are tender and the lamb is done to your liking (4–5 minutes per side for rare). To check for doneness, cut into a cube; the meat should be slightly less done than you like it.

When you put the lamb on the grill, rub the pitta breads with oil and sprinkle with sumac. Place them on the cooler side of the grill and cook until nicely toasted and slightly charred in a few places (2–3 minutes). Remove from the grill and cut each pitta bread into quarters.

When the lamb is done, push the kebabs off the skewers into a bowl, add the lemon juice, oil, oregano, and garlic, and toss gently to coat. Transfer to a serving plate and serve with the yogurt and toasted pittas.

SIRLOIN STEAK SKEWERS WITH AROMATIC HERBS, LIME, AND CHILLIES

In our experience, guests love interactive food – that is, food that they put together themselves. This appetizer, in which the intense flavours of Southeast Asia are combined with the familiar taste of beef, is a perfect example. We like it best set out on a table close to the grill, so guests can gather around and "roll their own" while you cook the main course.

Serves 4–6 as an appetizer

THE SKEWERS

450g (1lb) sirloin steak, cut into 1cm (½in) cubes
Kosher salt and freshly cracked black pepper

THE WRAPS

8–12 large lettuce leaves

THE DRESSING

Juice of 1 lime (about 2 tbsp)
1 tbsp soy sauce
1 tbsp Thai fish sauce (available in Asian markets or large supermarkets)
1 tbsp peeled and finely chopped fresh ginger
1 tbsp finely chopped fresh chilli peppers of your choice
1 tbsp roughly chopped fresh mint
1 tbsp roughly chopped fresh coriander
1 tbsp roughly chopped fresh basil

Build a fire in your grill. When the coals are all ignited, the flames have died down, and the temperature is hot (*see p34*), you're ready to cook.

Sprinkle the sirloin cubes generously with salt and pepper, thread them onto skewers, then put them on the grill directly over the coals and cook until they are just done (3–4 minutes per side for medium-rare). To check for doneness, poke the meat with your finger to test its firmness (*see p37*); if you're unsure, cut into one of the cubes to be sure it is slightly less done than you like it.

Push the cooked sirloin off the skewers into a large bowl, add all the dressing ingredients, and toss gently until the meat is evenly and thoroughly coated.

To serve, set out the sirloin cubes and the lettuce leaves on serving plates and pass them around, so that guests can "roll their own" beef and lettuce wraps.

SCALLOP KEBABS
WITH PINEAPPLE-CURRY RELISH

Scallops are great on the grill: easy, quick, and with a subtle but distinctive taste. If you make the relish in advance – which is no problem, because it will keep for four or five days in the refrigerator – this is about as fast a dish as you can imagine, yet it has plenty of interest and flavour.

Serves 4 as an appetizer

THE INGREDIENTS

450g (1lb) medium sea scallops (about 16 scallops)
2 tbsp olive oil
Kosher salt and freshly cracked black pepper
1 recipe Pineapple-Curry Relish (*see p189*)

Build a fire in your grill. When the coals are all ignited, the flames have died down, and the temperature is hot (*see p34*), you're ready to cook.

Rub the scallops with the olive oil and sprinkle them generously with salt and pepper. Thread the scallops onto skewers so that they lie flat, put them on the grill directly over the coals, and cook until they are just opaque throughout (3–4 minutes per side). To check for doneness, poke the scallops with your finger to test their firmness (*see p37*); if you're unsure, cut carefully into one of the scallops to be sure it is just opaque all the way through.

When the scallops are done, transfer the kebabs to a serving plate and serve, passing the relish on the side.

CHICKEN AND FIG KEBABS
WITH PARSLEY-PINE NUT RELISH

With jammy fresh figs and a relish that features rich pine nuts and the gentle astringency of parsley, this dish is a feast of Mediterranean flavours, despite its simplicity. If you can't find fresh figs, you can substitute firm but ripe apricots, halved.

Serves 4

THE INGREDIENTS

900g (2lb) boneless, skinless chicken breasts,
  cut into 2.5cm (1in) cubes
8 fresh ripe figs, halved lengthways
3 tbsp olive oil
Kosher salt and freshly cracked black pepper to taste
1 recipe Parsley Pine-Nut Relish (*see p262*)

Build a fire in your grill. When the coals are all ignited, the flames have died down, and the temperature is medium-hot (*see p34*), you're ready to cook.

Rub the chicken cubes and fig halves with the oil, sprinkle them generously with salt and pepper, and thread them alternately onto skewers so that the fig halves lie flat on their cut sides. Put them on the grill directly over the coals and cook until the figs are nicely browned and the chicken is just done (6–7 minutes per side). To check for doneness, cut into one of the cubes of chicken to be sure it is opaque right through.

When the kebabs are done, transfer them to a serving plate and serve, passing the relish on the side.

GRILLED LEMONGRASS CHICKEN GOUJONS WITH CHILLI-SOY DIPPING SAUCE

Chicken goujons are an excellent option for skewers. Small and tender, they cook quickly on the grill and provide a good foil for all kinds of strong flavours. The Asian-style dipping sauce we serve with them is delicious with any grilled chicken.

Serves 4 as an appetizer

THE SKEWERS

450g (1lb) chicken goujons, tendons removed (12–16 pieces)

3 stalks lemongrass, finely chopped (use the tender, inner portion of the bottom third only)

2 tbsp sesame oil

Kosher salt and freshly cracked white pepper to taste

THE SAUCE

150ml (5fl oz) soy sauce

4 tbsp hot chilli oil (available at most Asian grocery stores)

3 tbsp roughly chopped spring onions, white and green portions

2 tbsp peeled and finely chopped fresh ginger

1 tsp granulated sugar

Build a fire in your grill. When the coals are all ignited, the flames have died down, and the temperature is medium-hot (*see p34*), you're ready to cook.

Combine the sauce ingredients in a bowl and mix until the sugar dissolves. Transfer to a serving bowl and set aside.

Combine the chicken goujons, lemongrass, sesame oil, and salt and pepper in a bowl and toss until the chicken is evenly coated. Thread the chicken onto skewers, place on the grill directly over the coals, and cook until opaque throughout (3–4 minutes per side). To check for doneness, cut into one of the goujons to be sure that it is opaque all the way through.

When the goujons are done, arrange them on a serving plate along with the dipping sauce and serve immediately.

SPICY PORK SKEWERS

Alive with vibrant flavours, adobo spice paste is a quick way of adding a lot of flavour with little effort. Here we use it to coat strips of pork, which we then thread onto skewers like ribbons and cook quickly over a medium-hot fire. This is a perfect appetizer to serve before a light summer meal.

Serves 4 as an appetizer

THE INGREDIENTS

450g (1lb) boneless pork loin, cut into 16 equal strips
1 recipe Adobo Rub (*see p189*)
4 tbsp roughly chopped fresh coriander
2 limes, each cut in half

Build a fire in your grill. When the coals are all ignited, the flames have died down, and the temperature is medium-hot (*see p34*), you're ready to cook.

Rub the pork strips all over with the adobo rub, pressing gently to be sure that it adheres. Thread the pork onto skewers and grill until nicely browned but not charred (5–6 minutes per side for medium). To check for doneness, cut into one of the strips; it should be just slightly less done than you like it.

When the pork is done, transfer the skewers to a serving plate, sprinkle with the coriander, squeeze over the lime juice, and serve.

SALT AND PEPPER PRAWNS WITH HOT AND SOUR COLE SLAW

What we call Szechuan pepper is actually not a pepper at all; it is the dried berry of a prickly ash tree that grows widely in China. But whatever it may technically be, its tingling heat and unique citrus flavour are wonderful. We use it here to enliven grilled prawns, which we serve with a rather unusual slaw that features mung bean sprouts, an ingredient that has more potential than its often unimaginative use would suggest.

Serves 4 as an appetizer

THE SKEWERS

450g (1lb) raw prawns, 16/20 size, peeled and deveined

1 tbsp sesame oil

1 tbsp kosher salt

1 tbsp cracked Szechuan peppercorns

THE SLAW

250g (9oz) thinly sliced Chinese leaves

115g (4oz) mung bean sprouts

5 spring onions, including green tops, cut lengthways into thin strips

5 tbsp rice vinegar

3 tbsp soy sauce

2 tbsp granulated sugar

2 tbsp peeled and finely chopped fresh ginger

2 tbsp roughly chopped fresh mint

2 tbsp roughly chopped fresh coriander

2 tsp chilli pepper flakes

Kosher salt and freshly cracked white pepper to taste

Build a fire in your grill. When the coals are all ignited, the flames have died down, and the temperature is medium-hot (*see p34*), you're ready to cook.

Combine the prawns, sesame oil, salt, and Szechuan pepper in a large bowl, tossing to coat the prawns evenly. Thread the prawns onto 4 skewers, arrange them on the grill over the coals, and cook until just done (3–4 minutes per side). To check for doneness, cut into one of the prawns at its thickest point to be sure it is opaque all the way through.

While the prawns are cooking, combine the Chinese leaves, bean sprouts, and spring onions in a large bowl and toss until well mixed. In another bowl, combine the rice vinegar, soy sauce, sugar, ginger, mint, coriander and chilli pepper flakes, and mix well. Season the dressing to taste with salt and pepper. When the prawns are done, pour the dressing over the slaw and toss until it is well-coated. Divide the slaw among four salad plates and put a skewer of prawns on each one.

CURRIED DUCK SKEWERS WITH PINEAPPLE-GRAPE CHUTNEY

You don't often see duck on skewers, but it is actually very well-suited to this treatment. It is no harder to deal with than chicken, but you get a much richer flavour. Be careful not to overcook it, though; unlike chicken, it has the best flavour if served medium-rare or medium. If you don't happen to like the taste of sesame oil, you can simply substitute vegetable oil in this recipe.

Serves 4–6 as an appetizer

THE SKEWERS

450g (1lb) boneless duck breast (about 2 single breasts), most of the fat removed, cut into 16 slices

2 tbsp sesame oil

2 tbsp good-quality curry powder

1 tbsp kosher salt

1 tbsp freshly cracked black pepper

THE CHUTNEY

2 tbsp olive oil

1 small red onion, peeled and diced small

1 tbsp peeled and finely chopped fresh ginger

1 tbsp curry powder

150g (5½oz) diced fresh pineapple

85g (3oz) seedless red grapes, halved

120ml (4fl oz) cider vinegar

4 tbsp soft dark brown sugar

Kosher salt and freshly cracked black pepper to taste

Make the chutney: on the hob, heat the oil in a sauté pan over a medium-high heat until hot but not smoking. Add the onions and sauté, stirring occasionally, until transparent (7–9 minutes). Add the ginger and curry powder and continue to sauté, stirring frequently, until fragrant (about 1 minute more). Add the remaining ingredients and bring up to a simmer, stirring to dissolve the sugar. Adjust the heat to low and continue to simmer gently until slightly thickened (5–7 minutes). Remove from the heat, season with salt and pepper, and allow to cool to room temperature before serving. (This chutney will keep, covered and refrigerated, for 4–5 days.)

Build a fire in your grill. When the coals are all ignited, the flames have died down, and the temperature is medium-hot (*see p34*), you're ready to cook.

Rub the duck strips with sesame oil and sprinkle them with the curry powder, salt, and pepper. Thread the duck onto skewers, place on the grill directly over the coals, and cook until nicely browned but not charred (5–7 minutes per side). To check for doneness, cut into one of the duck strips to be sure it is just slightly less done than you like it, to account for carryover cooking. (We like duck breast medium-rare to medium.)

When the duck is done, transfer the skewers to a serving plate and serve, passing the chutney on the side.

FLAVOUR FOOTPRINT CHINA

In many ways, of course, it is ridiculous to talk about a single flavour footprint for a country as huge, with cuisines as varied, as China. But in fact there are a handful of ingredients that, when combined in a dish, evoke the cooking of this country, at least to Western taste buds. Five-spice powder, sesame oil, hoisin sauce, Szechuan peppercorns, and star anise are probably the most distinctive of these, perhaps because they all either originated or were first created in China. With one or two of these easy seasonings at hand, you can effortlessly expand your flavour horizon.

All-Purpose Ginger-Soy Barbecue Sauce
Makes about 500ml (16fl oz)

You can use this sauce either as a last-minute finishing glaze or as an accompanying dipping sauce for pretty much anything grilled, from beef to lamb to chicken to vegetables.

120ml (4fl oz) tomato ketchup
120ml (4fl oz) hoisin sauce
120ml (4fl oz) soy sauce
60ml (2fl oz) rice wine vinegar
3 tbsp peeled and finely chopped fresh ginger

Combine all the ingredients in a small bowl and mix well. This sauce will keep, covered and refrigerated, for about a week.

Aromatic Rub

Aromatic Rub
Makes about 115g (4oz)

This fragrant, dry spice rub is wonderful rubbed on chicken or pork before grilling.

4 tbsp ground coriander
2 tbsp ground white pepper
2 tbsp ground Szechuan peppercorns
2 tbsp mustard powder
2 tbsp ground ginger
1 tbsp kosher salt
1 tsp cinnamon

Combine all the ingredients in a small bowl and mix well. Stored in an airtight container and kept in a cool, dark place, this rub will last for a month or longer.

All-Purpose Ginger-
Soy Barbecue Sauce

Orange-Ginger Soy Sauce with Coriander

Makes about 200ml (8fl oz)

We serve this as a sauce partner for just about anything grilled.

120ml (4fl oz) soy sauce
1 tbsp freshly squeezed orange juice
1 tbsp grated orange zest
1 tbsp finely chopped fresh ginger
2 tbsp rice wine vinegar
2 tbsp finely chopped fresh coriander
1 tsp granulated sugar
Pinch of ground white pepper

Combine all the ingredients in a small bowl and mix well until the sugar dissolves. This sauce will keep, covered and refrigerated, for 2–3 days.

Sesame-Ginger Paste

Makes about 115g (4oz)

Try rubbing this paste on steak, pork chops, or chicken just before they go on the grill.

5 tbsp peeled and finely chopped fresh ginger
4 tbsp sesame oil
2 tbsp roughly chopped spring onions, with green tops
1 tbsp finely chopped fresh garlic
1 tbsp finely chopped fresh chilli pepper of your choice
1 tbsp freshly cracked white pepper

Combine all the ingredients in a small bowl and mix well. This paste will keep, covered and refrigerated, for 3–4 days.

SIGNATURE INGREDIENTS/TOP ROW (LEFT TO RIGHT) Five-spice powder, sesame oil, soy sauce;
SECOND ROW Ginger, chilli sauce, rice wine vinegar;
THIRD ROW Sesame seeds, star anise, white peppercorns;
BOTTOM ROW Hoisin sauce, garlic, Szechuan pepper.

Sesame-Water Chestnut Relish

Makes about 200g (7oz)

This fragrant, crunchy relish is lovely served alongside grilled fish or chicken.

2 tbsp sesame seeds
115g (4oz) canned water chestnuts, diced medium
3 tbsp roughly chopped spring onions, with green tops
2 tbsp sesame oil
1 tbsp peeled and finely chopped fresh ginger

Toast the sesame seeds on the hob in a dry frying pan over a medium heat, shaking them frequently to avoid burning, until they are fragrant and just a shade darker. Combine all the ingredients in a medium bowl and mix well. This will keep, covered and refrigerated, for 2 days.

Sesame-Water Chestnut Relish

GLAZED PORK AND APPLE SKEWERS

Pork and apples make a classic combination; we both first experienced it as children when our grandmothers served us roast pork accompanied by home-made apple sauce. Here we put them over the coals, then brush them with a simple but lively glaze enlivened with the liquorice-y flavour of caraway. The glaze takes a little while to reduce down, but otherwise, this is a very quick dish to prepare. You could, if you think of it, make the glaze ahead of time, when you're in the kitchen doing something else, anyway. It will keep, covered and refrigerated, for weeks.

Serves 4

THE SKEWERS

900g (2lb) pork tenderloin, cut into 2.5cm (1in) cubes

2 Granny Smith or other green apples, cored, each cut into 8 wedges

3 tbsp olive oil

Kosher salt and freshly cracked black pepper to taste

THE GLAZE

360ml (12fl oz) fresh orange juice

120ml (4fl oz) balsamic vinegar

1 tbsp caraway seed

1 tsp freshly cracked black pepper

Combine the glaze ingredients in a small saucepan and bring to the boil. Reduce the heat to medium and simmer vigorously until the mixture has been reduced by two-thirds and become syrupy (30–40 minutes). Leave to cool.

Meanwhile, build a fire in your grill. When the coals are all ignited, the flames have died down, and the temperature is medium-hot (see p34), you're ready to cook.

Combine the pork, apple wedges, oil, and salt and pepper in a large bowl, and toss gently until evenly coated. Thread the pork and apples alternately onto skewers, put them on the grill directly over the coals, and cook until the apples are golden and slightly softened and the pork is just done (5–6 minutes per side for medium). Brush with the glaze during the last minute of cooking. To check for doneness, poke the pork cubes with your finger to test their firmness (see p37); if you're unsure, cut into one to be sure it is just slightly less done than you like it, to account for carryover cooking.

When the skewers are ready, arrange them on a serving plate, drizzle with some of the remaining glaze, and serve.

SWORDFISH SHISH KEBAB
WITH MANGO-GINGER RELISH

Although in Turkey, where the term comes from, "shish kebab" means anything grilled on a skewer, in the US it has come to denote the particular arrangement of cubes of meat alternating on a skewer with peppers and onions. Here we substitute swordfish steak for the beef, which gives the kebab a more delicate flavour. Fortunately, this fish has a firm enough texture to stand up to the treatment.

Serves 4

THE INGREDIENTS

900g (2lb) swordfish steak, about 2.5cm (1in) thick, cut into 2.5cm (1in) cubes

2 red peppers, cored, deseeded, and halved, each half quartered

1 red onion, peeled and halved, each half quartered

4 tbsp olive oil

Kosher salt and freshly cracked black pepper to taste

1 recipe Mango-Ginger Relish (*see p115*)

Build a fire in your grill. When the coals are all ignited, the flames have died down, and the temperature is medium-hot (*see p34*), you're ready to cook.

Combine the swordfish, red peppers, onion, oil, and salt and pepper in a large bowl and toss until evenly coated. Thread the fish, red peppers, and onion alternately onto skewers, put them on the grill directly over the coals, and cook until the vegetables are tender and the swordfish is just done (4–5 minutes per side). To check for doneness, poke the fish with your finger to test its firmness (*see p37*); if you're unsure, cut into one of the cubes; it should be just opaque throughout.

When the skewers are done, transfer them to a serving plate and serve, passing the relish on the side.

LAMB KEBABS WITH CUCUMBER-FETA RELISH

Although the flavours of this dish are most closely identified with Greece, it seems a little Persian as well, with the lushly aromatic peaches and the meaty, slightly sweet lamb. If you're lucky enough to have any leftovers, you can make a very delicious sandwich by piling everything into a pitta bread.

Serves 4

THE KEBABS

900g (2lb) boneless leg of lamb, cut into 2.5cm (1in) cubes

2 ripe but firm peaches, stoned and cut into eighths

2 red peppers, cored, deseeded, and halved, each half quartered

1 red onion, peeled and halved, each half quartered

4 tbsp olive oil

1 tbsp finely chopped garlic

1 tbsp dried oregano

Kosher salt and freshly cracked black pepper to taste

THE RELISH

1 cucumber, peeled and diced small

225g (8oz) feta cheese, diced medium

4 tbsp roughly chopped fresh mint

4 tbsp extra virgin olive oil

2 tbsp red wine vinegar

Kosher salt and freshly cracked black pepper to taste

Build a fire in your grill. When the coals are all ignited, the flames have died down, and the temperature is medium-hot (see p34), you're ready to cook.

Combine the lamb, peaches, red peppers, onion, oil, garlic, oregano, and salt and pepper in a large bowl and toss gently. Thread the lamb, peach, red pepper, and onion alternately onto skewers, place on the grill directly over the coals, and cook until the vegetables are tender and the meat is just done (4–5 minutes per side for rare). To check for doneness, poke the lamb with your finger to test its firmness (see p37); if you're unsure, cut into one of the cubes and check that it is slightly less done than you like it, to account for carryover cooking.

While the kebabs cook, combine the relish ingredients in a medium-sized bowl and toss gently to combine.

When the kebabs are ready, transfer them to a serving plate and serve, passing the relish on the side.

SALADS FROM THE GRILL

FRESH, VIBRANT, AND JUST A LITTLE UNUSUAL, SALADS THAT INCLUDE GRILLED FOOD MAKE GREAT APPETIZERS, EXCELLENT SIDE DISHES, EVEN SATISFYING LIGHT MEALS. NOT TO MENTION THAT THEY'RE PRETTY GOOD FOR YOU

STEAK AND TOMATO OPEN SANDWICHES

Okay, so maybe this isn't precisely a sandwich. In fact, it's sort of a grilled steak kebab salad, featuring lightly grilled cherry tomatoes, that you pile on top of thick slices of grilled bread. But when you get a bite of that rich, meaty sirloin along with the fresh-tasting vinaigrette and the crusty bread with the tomato juices soaked into it, you're really not going to care what it's called. It's just plain delicious.

Serves 4

THE SALAD

900g (2lb) sirloin steak, cut into 3.5cm (1½in) cubes
2 tbsp vegetable oil
2 tbsp freshly cracked cumin seeds (or substitute
  1 tbsp ground cumin)
Kosher salt and freshly cracked black pepper to taste
16 cherry tomatoes
4 slices of good French bread, about 2.5cm (1in)
  thick

THE DRESSING

½ small red onion, peeled and diced small
15g (½oz) roughly chopped fresh parsley
5 tbsp extra virgin olive oil
4 tbsp balsamic vinegar
1 tbsp finely chopped fresh garlic
3–6 dashes of Tabasco sauce, or to taste
Kosher salt and freshly cracked black pepper to taste

Build a fire in your grill. When the coals are all ignited, the flames have died down, and the temperature is medium-hot (*see p34*), you're ready to cook.

Combine the vinaigrette ingredients in a large bowl, mix well, and set aside.

Combine the sirloin cubes, oil, cumin, and salt and pepper in a large bowl and toss until the beef is evenly coated. Thread the cubes onto skewers, put them on the grill directly over the coals, and cook until they are just done (5–7 minutes per side for medium-rare). To check for doneness, poke the meat with your finger to test its firmness (*see p37*); if you're unsure, cut into one of the cubes; it should be slightly less done than you like it.

While the meat is cooking, thread the cherry tomatoes onto skewers, put them on the grill next to the meat, and cook just until the tomatoes are lightly coloured but not cooked through (about 2 minutes per side). Arrange the bread slices around the perimeter of the fire and cook until lightly toasted (about 2 minutes per side).

When the meat and the tomatoes are done, gently push them off their skewers into the bowl containing the vinaigrette, then toss gently to coat.

To serve, place a slice of toast on each plate, spoon the sirloin and tomatoes evenly over each slice, and serve immediately.

GRILLED PRAWN, WATERCRESS, AND MANGO SALAD WITH SESAME-SOY DRESSING

The combination of peppery greens, lush grilled prawns, and sweet fruit gives you a very flavourful, interesting salad that is both substantial and refreshing. Here we serve it with a slightly piquant dressing that combines a range of wonderful Asian flavours. You can leave out the fish sauce if you like, but the dressing will not have as deep a flavour.

Serves 4 as a salad course or appetizer

THE SALAD

450g (1lb) extra large raw prawns, peeled
2 tbsp vegetable oil
1 tbsp five-spice powder
Kosher salt and freshly cracked black pepper to taste
2 bunches watercress, trimmed, washed, and dried
2 ripe but firm mangoes, peeled, stoned, and cut into chunks

THE DRESSING

4 tbsp extra virgin olive oil
4 tbsp sesame oil
4 tbsp soy sauce
2 tbsp distilled white vinegar
2 tbsp peeled and finely chopped fresh ginger
1 tsp granulated sugar
4 dashes of Tabasco sauce
2 tbsp Thai fish sauce (available in Asian markets or large supermarkets)

Build a fire in your grill. When the coals are all ignited, the flames have died down, and the temperature is medium-hot (*see p34*), you're ready to cook.

Combine all the dressing ingredients in a small bowl, whisk to blend well, then set aside.

Rub the prawns with oil, sprinkle with five-spice powder, salt, and pepper, and thread onto skewers. Put them over the coals and grill until they are opaque all the way through (3–4 minutes per side), then remove from the grill and allow to cool to room temperature (about 15 minutes).

Put the watercress in a large bowl, slide the grilled shrimp off the skewers onto the watercress, then add the mangoes. Whisk the dressing again to blend, add just enough to moisten the salad (there will probably be some dressing left over), toss well, and serve.

SPINACH AND PEACH SALAD WITH BLUE CHEESE, BACON, AND SWEET-AND-SOUR DRESSING

If you've never had grilled fruit before, peaches are a perfect introduction; just a few minutes over the coals adds a trace of smoky char that is the perfect complement to their natural sweetness. Put them together with fresh spinach and a crumble of blue cheese and bacon, and you've got a salad (*see overleaf*) that is fantastic on its own but also makes a great appetizer before a simple steak dinner.

Serves 4 as a salad course or appetizer

THE SALAD

8 streaky bacon rashers

2 ripe but firm peaches, halved and stoned

2 tbsp olive oil

2 bunches baby spinach leaves, trimmed, washed, and dried

60g (2oz) crumbled blue cheese of your choice

THE DRESSING

2 tbsp tomato ketchup

2 tbsp wholegrain mustard

1 tbsp granulated sugar

1 tsp finely chopped fresh garlic

180ml (6floz) extra virgin olive oil

4 tbsp balsamic vinegar

Juice of I lime (about 2 tbsp)

Kosher salt and freshly cracked black pepper to taste

Build a fire in your grill. When the coals are all ignited, the flames have died down, and the temperature is medium-hot (*see p34*), you're ready to cook.

On the hob, cook the bacon in a sauté pan over medium heat until crisp (6–8 minutes). Drain off any fat and let the bacon cool until you are able to handle it, then crumble it roughly between your fingers into a small bowl.

Make the dressing: combine the ketchup, mustard, sugar, and garlic in a blender or food processor and purée. With the machine running, add the oil in a slow, steady stream. When all the oil is incorporated, add the vinegar and lime juice and pulse to combine. Season with salt and pepper to taste.

Rub the peach halves with oil, sprinkle them with salt and pepper, then put over the coals and grill, cut-sides down, until nicely browned (4–5 minutes). Remove from the grill, cut each half into 4 wedges, and transfer to a large bowl, along with the spinach.

Pulse the dressing a few more times to blend; add enough dressing to the peaches and spinach just to moisten (there will probably be some dressing left over), and toss to coat. Arrange the salad on a serving plate or individual plates, sprinkle generously with the blue cheese and bacon, and serve.

SMOKY AUBERGINE AND PEPPER SALAD WITH ROAST GARLIC, POMEGRANATE MOLASSES, AND MINT

If you look at American cuisine, you might think that the idea of grilling vegetables was invented in the 1980s. But in the Middle East there is an ancient and enduring relationship between vegetables and live fire. This substantial salad is in the *mezze* tradition of that part of the world, and uses some of its classic flavours. If you already have a fire going, you can ash-roast the garlic in advance, wrapped in a double layer of foil (*see* Hobo Packs, *p302*); otherwise, roast it gently in the oven for that authentic taste and texture.

Serves 4 as a salad course or appetizer

THE SALAD

2 medium aubergines, sliced into rounds about 1cm (½in) thick
2 red peppers, cored, deseeded, and halved
4 tbsp olive oil
Kosher salt and freshly cracked black pepper to taste
2 pitta breads
2 tbsp extra virgin olive oil
1 tbsp freshly cracked coriander seeds (or substitute 1½ tsp ground coriander)

THE DRESSING

1 head of garlic
Juice of 1 lemon (about 4 tbsp)
5 tbsp extra virgin olive oil
4 tbsp roughly chopped fresh mint
2 tbsp pomegranate molasses (or substitute treacle)
1 tsp ground cumin
Kosher salt and freshly cracked black pepper to taste

Roast the garlic for the dressing: heat the oven to 150°C (300°F); slice the top quarter off the head, set it on a sheet of foil and sprinkle with a little oil, salt, and pepper, then wrap and roast until soft (about 1 hour).

Build a multilevel fire in your grill (*see p31*). When the coals are all ignited, the flames have died down, and the temperature is medium-hot (*see p34*), you're ready to cook.

In a large bowl, combine the aubergines, red peppers, oil, and salt and pepper and toss gently. Put the vegetables on the hotter side of the grill and cook, turning once, until slightly browned (4–5 minutes per side for the aubergine; 3–4 minutes per side for the peppers). Put them back into the bowl you originally tossed them in.

While the vegetables cook, rub the pitta breads with oil, sprinkle with coriander, and place on the side of the grill with fewer coals. Cook until nicely toasted and slightly charred here and there (2–3 minutes). Cut into wedges.

Make the dressing: making sure the garlic is cool enough to handle, squeeze the flesh from each clove and mash with the lemon juice in a small bowl. Add the remaining ingredients and mix well. Pour the dressing over the vegetables and toss gently. Transfer the salad to a serving dish and serve, accompanied by the grilled pitta bread.

CHILLI PRAWN, COS LETTUCE, AND AVOCADO SALAD WITH LIME-CUMIN DRESSING

This salad is our tribute to Caesar Cardini, the Mexican restaurateur who is credited with inventing in 1924 what today is the single most popular salad in the United States – the Caesar. While this one is quite different, its crunchy texture and the Mexican flavours of lime, coriander, cumin, chilli, and avocado make it equally appealing.

Serves 4 as a salad course or appetizer

THE SALAD

450g (1lb) raw prawns, 16/20 size, peeled
2 tbsp olive oil
1 tsp chilli powder
Kosher salt and freshly cracked black pepper to taste
1 large head cos lettuce, washed, dried, and cut crossways into 5cm (2in) pieces
12 cherry tomatoes, washed, dried, and stemmed
2 ripe but firm avocados, halved, stoned, peeled, and each half cut into 3 wedges

THE DRESSING

Juice of 3 limes (about 5 tbsp)
5 tbsp extra virgin olive oil
2 tbsp roughly chopped fresh coriander
1 tsp finely chopped fresh garlic
1 tsp ground cumin
Kosher salt and freshly cracked black pepper to taste

Build a fire in your grill. When the coals are all ignited, the flames have died down, and the temperature is medium-hot (*see p34*), you're ready to cook.

In a large bowl, whisk the dressing ingredients together well.

In another bowl, combine the prawns, oil, chilli powder, and salt and pepper and mix well to coat the prawns evenly. If desired, thread the prawns onto skewers; otherwise, arrange them on the hot side of the grill. Cook until just done (3–4 minutes per side). To check for doneness, carefully cut into one of the prawns at its thickest point and peek inside to be sure it is just opaque all the way through.

While the prawns are cooking, divide the lettuce, cherry tomatoes, and avocado wedges among four salad plates.

Transfer the cooked prawns to the bowl of dressing (pushing them off the skewers, if you used them) and mix gently. Arrange the prawns on each salad, spoon the remaining dressing over the top, and serve.

SPAIN: DISCOVERING SMALL BITES

We first came across tapas nearly 30 years ago in the tiny, somewhat decrepit working-class bars of Madrid. We walked into the first of these minuscule "joints" – nothing more than a long, narrow bar with a few stools and some standing room – at random, in search of a mid-afternoon beer.

At first we were puzzled by the fact that the floor was literally covered, like a carpet of fallen leaves, with scraps of paper. Then we discovered the primary pastime of the patrons: gambling. For a couple of pesetas, you bought little slips of paper and tore them open to see if you had won anything. Imitating the regulars at the bar, we bought them by the handful and sat there opening them and throwing them away like so many peanut shells. And, like everyone else, we accompanied our triumphs and disappointments with many little glasses of beer or Rioja and an endless succession of the savoury snacks known as tapas that were lined up on the bar, each impaled with a toothpick. Oddly, each time we ate one and discarded the toothpick, we noticed that the bartender would carefully place a clean toothpick on a plate in front of us. After many quizzical looks and shrugs of the shoulders, we finally figured out that he calculated the bill according to the pile of toothpicks in front of you, each tapas costing exactly the same. A chunk of spicy chorizo, a trio of smoky arbequina olives, a fresh fig topped with a smidgen of Cabrales cheese, a single slice of acorn-fed ham – each was a tiny treat of intense, deep flavour. Today tapas are globally known and immensely popular. Wherever I find them, though, they always take me back to those lazy, innocent afternoons of what we like to think of as true cultural exploration.

GRILLED FIGS
WITH BLUE CHEESE AND CRISPY HAM

We love the rich flavour and jammy texture of grilled figs, here perfectly matched with tangy blue cheese and lightly crisped ham. For the most Spanish-tasting dish, use Serrano ham and Cabrales cheese. If they're not available, though, you can use Parma ham and any good-quality blue cheese. Our friends Valerie and Ihsan Gurdal, of Formaggio Kitchen in Boston and New York, insist that you should use whatever variety of blue cheese is made closest to you; we're sure that, as usual, they're right.

Serves 4 as an appetizer

8 fresh ripe figs, halved lengthways
2 tbsp olive oil
Kosher salt and freshly cracked black pepper to taste
8 slices Serrano ham (or substitute Parma ham), halved lengthways into strips
115g (4oz) Cabrales or other blue cheese of your choice, crumbled

Build a fire in your grill. When the coals are all ignited, the flames have died down, and the temperature is medium (*see p34*), you're ready to cook.

Toss the figs with the olive oil in a medium bowl and sprinkle with salt and pepper. Place on the grill directly over the coals, cut-side down, and cook until just nicely browned (3–4 minutes).

Put the ham on the grill directly over the coals and cook just until crisp (about 1 minute).

Top each fig with some of the cheese and the crisp ham. Serve warm or at room temperature.

THAI CHICKEN AND CHINESE CABBAGE SALAD WITH PEANUT-LIME DRESSING

Cooks in the tropical world have a tendency to turn to cabbage for their salads, since it holds up better in hot weather than more tender greens. We like it because it has a nice little bite to it, and also has a great crunchy consistency. Here it provides the perfect foil for a lively peanut-lime dressing and grilled chicken breasts given mouth-searing tropical heat with a rub of chillies and white pepper.

Serves 4 as a main course

THE SALAD

- 2–4 tbsp finely chopped fresh chilli peppers of your choice, to taste
- 2 tbsp freshly cracked white pepper (or substitute black pepper)
- 3 tbsp kosher salt
- 4 boneless, skinless chicken breasts, sliced in half crossways, about 225g (8oz) each
- ½ head Chinese cabbage, cut crossways into thin strips
- 1 red pepper, halved, seeded, and cut into thin strips
- 15g (½oz) fresh basil leaves
- 15g (½oz) fresh coriander leaves
- 15g (½oz) fresh mint leaves

THE DRESSING

- Juice of 2 limes (about 4 tbsp)
- 3 tbsp Thai fish sauce (available in Asian markets or large supermarkets)
- 2 tbsp finely chopped unsalted roasted peanuts
- 1 tbsp granulated sugar
- 1 tbsp peeled and finely chopped fresh ginger
- 1 tsp finely chopped fresh garlic

Build a fire in your grill. When the coals are all ignited, the flames have died down, and the temperature is medium-hot (*see p34*), you're ready to cook.

Combine all the dressing ingredients in a small bowl, whisk to blend well, then set aside.

Combine the chopped chillies, white pepper, and salt in another small bowl and mix well. Rub the chicken generously with this spice mixture, then put it over the coals and grill until opaque all the way through (6–8 minutes per side, depending on thickness). To check for doneness, cut into one piece and peek in to be sure that it is opaque all the way through. Set the chicken aside to cool slightly.

Combine the cabbage, red pepper, and herbs in a large bowl. Slice the chicken crossways into thin strips, then cut the slices into bite-sized pieces and add to the salad. Stir the dressing again, add just enough to moisten the salad (there will probably be some dressing left over), toss to coat, and serve.

LATIN-STYLE CABBAGE SALAD
WITH GRILLED PORK AND PINEAPPLE SKEWERS

This main course salad is inspired by our favourite version of the classic Costa Rican lunch known as *casado*, which consists of a cabbage salad, a piece of pork, and some rice and beans. Here we've put the pork right into the salad and added pineapple for sweetness and texture. We admit that we've cheated a bit by adding the chipotle, which is really Mexican, but we think its smoky heat is the perfect complement to the grilled fruit and meat.

Serves 4

THE SALAD

1 pork tenderloin, about 350–400g (12–14oz), trimmed and cut into 2cm (½in) cubes

1 small or ½ large ripe pineapple, peeled and cut into 2cm (½in) cubes

2 tbsp olive oil

Kosher salt and freshly cracked black pepper to taste

3 tbsp cumin seeds

1 small head green cabbage, cored and diced large

1 red pepper, deseeded and diced medium

1 carrot, peeled and diced medium

20g (¾oz) fresh coriander leaves

THE DRESSING

240ml (8fl oz) pineapple juice or orange juice

180ml (6fl oz) extra virgin olive oil

Juice of 2 limes (about 4 tbsp)

3 tbsp finely chopped canned or bottled chipotle peppers in adobo sauce

1 tbsp finely chopped fresh garlic

Kosher salt and freshly cracked black pepper to taste

Make the dressing: on the hob, bring the fruit juice to the boil in a small pan over a high heat, then lower the heat and simmer until reduced to a syrupy consistency (25–30 minutes). Remove from the heat and allow to cool to room temperature. Add the olive oil, lime juice, chipotles, garlic, and salt and pepper, mix well, and set aside.

Build a fire in your grill. When the coals are all ignited, the flames have died down, and the temperature is medium (*see p34*), you're ready to cook.

Combine the pork and pineapple cubes in a large bowl, add the oil and salt and pepper, and toss to coat. Thread the cubes alternately onto skewers, then put over the coals and grill until the pork is well-seared and done to your liking (5–6 minutes per side for medium). To check for doneness, cut into one of the pork cubes; the meat should be just slightly less done than you like it. Set the skewers aside to cool slightly.

Toast the cumin seeds in a dry frying pan over the fire (or on the hob over a medium heat), shaking them frequently to prevent burning, until they become fragrant and just a shade darker (3–5 minutes).

Combine the cabbage, red pepper, carrot, and coriander in a large bowl. Push the pork and pineapple off the skewers into the bowl. Stir the dressing again, add just enough to moisten the salad ingredients (there will probably be some left over), and toss to coat. Sprinkle the toasted cumin seeds over the salad and serve.

CURRIED CHICKEN SALAD WITH WATERCRESS, GRAPES, AND PEACHES

As you cook the curry-coated chicken in this dish, the marvellous aroma that rises up from the grill will give you a clear idea of how the heat brings out the flavour of spices. It's important to use a good curry powder here, since the lesser ones can have a chalky quality. To balance the spiciness of the curry, we add sweet grapes and peaches along with pleasantly bitter watercress for an exciting flavour trio.

Serves 4 as a salad course or appetizer

THE SALAD

2 boneless, skinless chicken breasts, about 225g (8oz) each, split horizontally

2 tbsp olive oil

1 tbsp good-quality curry powder

Kosher salt and freshly cracked black pepper

2 bunches watercress, trimmed, washed, and dried well

20 seedless green grapes, halved

2 ripe but firm peaches, stoned and sliced into eighths

THE DRESSING

240ml (8fl oz) fresh orange juice

5 tbsp extra virgin olive oil

5 tbsp red wine vinegar

2 tbsp roughly chopped fresh parsley

Kosher salt and freshly cracked black pepper to taste

Make the dressing: on the hob, bring the orange juice to the boil in a small pan over a high heat, then lower the heat slightly and simmer until reduced in volume to 4 tbsp (about 20 minutes). Remove from the heat and allow to cool to room temperature. Add the oil, wine vinegar, parsley, salt, and pepper, whisk together, and set aside.

Build a fire in your grill. When the coals are all ignited, the flames have died down, and the temperature is medium (see p34), you're ready to cook.

Coat the chicken breasts with oil, rub them all over with the curry powder, and sprinkle them generously with salt and pepper. Place them on the grill directly over the coals and cook until they are browned on the outside and just cooked through (6–8 minutes per side). To check for doneness, poke the chicken with your finger to test its firmness (see p37); if you're unsure, make a cut in the thickest part of one of the breasts and check to be sure that it is opaque all the way through. When the breasts are done, transfer them to a plate and cover them loosely with foil to keep warm.

While the chicken is cooking, combine the watercress, grapes, and peaches in a large bowl. Stir the dressing again, add to the watercress-fruit mixture, and toss well to coat. Divide the salad among four plates.

Slice the chicken diagonally into strips, arrange the strips on top of each salad, and serve.

ARTICHOKE, ROCKET, AND RADICCHIO SALAD WITH LEMON-FETA DRESSING

To us, artichokes have a rather meaty flavour, which makes them a natural for the grill. The slight bitterness of the rocket and radicchio in this salad provides a good complement to the mellowness of the artichoke, and the Greek flavours of the dressing bring it all together.

Serves 4 as a salad course or appetizer

THE SALAD

4 globe artichokes
1 red pepper, cored, deseeded, and halved
1 small red onion, peeled and sliced in 1cm (½in) thick rounds (keep rings together)
4 tbsp olive oil
Kosher salt and freshly cracked black pepper
1 bunch rocket, trimmed, washed, and dried well
1 head radicchio, cored and sliced into thin strips

THE DRESSING

60g (2oz) crumbled feta cheese
5 tbsp extra virgin olive oil
Juice of 1 lemon (about 4 tbsp)
2 tbsp roughly chopped fresh parsley
1 tsp finely chopped fresh garlic
Kosher salt and freshly cracked black pepper to taste

On the hob, bring a large pan of salted water to the boil over a high heat. While the water is heating, trim the artichoke stems, snap off the coarse outer leaves, then cut 2.5cm (1in) off the top of each artichoke. Quarter each artichoke and remove the hairy-looking "choke" from each quarter. Add the artichoke quarters to the boiling water, adjust the heat to low, and simmer until tender (15–20 minutes). Drain, cool in a bowl of ice water, and drain well again. Set aside.

Build a fire in your grill. When the coals are all ignited, the flames have died down, and the temperature is hot (*see p34*), you're ready to cook.

Rub the poached artichoke hearts, red pepper, and onion slices with oil and sprinkle generously with salt and pepper. Put the vegetables on the grill and cook until golden-brown and slightly charred (5–7 minutes per side). Transfer the grilled artichoke hearts and onions to a large bowl, separating the onions into rings; cut the grilled peppers into strips and add them to the bowl, along with the rocket and radicchio.

Whisk together all the dressing ingredients in a medium bowl (the dressing will be chunky). Add the dressing to the salad gradually, tossing very gently as you go along until everything is lightly and evenly coated.

PEPPER-CRUSTED FLANK STEAK SALAD
WITH TOMATO AND BASIL

On those hot summer days when you want a meal that is light but still satisfying, this Mediterranean-inspired salad is the perfect solution. It's particularly good in late summer when tomatoes are at their peak and basil is most flavourful. Be sure to cut the flank steak very thin and diagonally, so it is nice and tender.

Serves 4 as a main course

THE SALAD

4 tbsp freshly cracked black pepper
3 tbsp kosher salt
450g (1lb) flank steak or topside
1 bunch rocket, trimmed, washed, and dried
45g (1½oz) small fresh basil leaves
4 vine-ripened tomatoes (preferably beefsteak), about the size of tennis balls, cored and sliced about 2.5cm (1in) thick

THE DRESSING

5 tbsp top-quality extra virgin olive oil
3 tbsp top-quality balsamic vinegar
Kosher salt and freshly cracked black pepper to taste

Build a fire in your grill. When the coals are all ignited, the flames have died down, and the temperature is hot (*see p34*), you're ready to cook.

Combine the 4 tbsp black pepper and 3 tbsp salt in a small bowl and mix well. Rub the steak generously with this mixture, lay it over the coals, and grill until almost done to your taste (5–7 minutes per side, depending on thickness, for medium-rare). To check for doneness, poke the steak with your finger to test its firmness (*see p37*); if you're unsure, make a cut in the thickest part and peek inside to be sure that it is slightly less done than you like it. Set the steak aside to cool slightly.

Scatter the rocket and basil leaves over a large serving plate to cover. Lay the tomato slices on top. Slice the steak crossways as thinly as possible, then cut the slices in half and arrange them over the tomatoes. Drizzle the oil over the salad, followed by the balsamic vinegar, then sprinkle generously with salt and pepper and serve immediately.

FLAVOUR FOOTPRINT
EASTERN MEDITERRANEAN-NORTH AFRICA

There are important distinctions among the many cuisines of the eastern Mediterranean and North Africa. However, they do all share a basic approach to flavour, as well as many common ingredients. Nuts are very prevalent in these cuisines, as are honey, a wide range of highly aromatic, often floral spices, and many types of ground dried chillies, from relatively mild to quite hot. We think these cuisines are poised to skyrocket in popularity, and this handful of make-ahead flavouring dishes lets you bring their exotic allure to your own table.

North African Chilli Paste
Makes about 180g (6oz)

This all-purpose chilli paste will accompany almost anything perfectly – or use it as a wet rub for chicken or pork just before you grill them.

4 tbsp dried red chilli peppers, finely crushed
2 tbsp coriander seeds, crushed
2 tbsp finely chopped fresh garlic
1 tbsp cumin seed
1 tbsp caraway seed
1 tbsp kosher salt
1 tbsp freshly cracked black pepper
5 tbsp vegetable oil

Combine all the ingredients in a small bowl, or, if you prefer a finer paste, mash in a pestle and mortar. This paste will keep, covered and refrigerated, for 2–3 days.

Parsley-Pine Nut Relish
Makes about 115g (4oz)

Great served as an accompaniment for lamb, chicken, or fish, or sprinkled on grilled vegetables.

5 tbsp pine nuts
5 tbsp roughly chopped fresh parsley
4 tbsp extra virgin olive oil
1 tbsp finely chopped lemon zest
1 tsp finely chopped fresh garlic
Kosher salt and freshly cracked black pepper to taste

Toast the pine nuts in a shallow baking tin in a 180°C (350°F/Gas 4) oven until they are golden (5–10 minutes), or in a dry frying pan over a medium heat for 2–3 minutes, shaking frequently to avoid burning. Combine all the ingredients in a small bowl and mix well. This relish is best used the day it is made, but it will keep, covered and refrigerated, for 3 days.

North African
Chilli Paste

Peach Relish with Cumin and Mint
Makes about 280g (10oz)

Try this as an accompaniment to grilled chicken, fish, or pork.

2 large, ripe but firm peaches, pitted and diced small
4 tbsp roughly chopped fresh mint
Juice of 1 lemon (about 4 tbsp)
2 tbsp cumin seeds
Kosher salt and freshly cracked black pepper to taste

Combine all the ingredients in a medium bowl and mix well. This relish will keep, covered and refrigerated, for 3–4 days.

Dill-Pomegranate Butter
Makes about 140g (5oz)

Put a dab or chilled slice of this on chicken or fish when it comes off the grill.

115g (4oz) unsalted butter, softened
2 tbsp pomegranate seeds
1 tbsp roughly chopped fresh dill
Kosher salt and freshly cracked black pepper to taste

Combine all the ingredients in a small bowl and mash together until evenly blended. This butter will keep, wrapped in greaseproof paper and refrigerated, for about 1 week. (Because of the fresh pomegranate seeds, it does not freeze well.)

SIGNATURE INGREDIENTS/TOP ROW (LEFT TO RIGHT)
Cardamom, walnuts, dried chillies, dill; **SECOND ROW** Saffron, sumac, cinnamon, pistachio nuts; **THIRD ROW** Dried limes, oregano, pine nuts, pomegranate molasses; **BOTTOM ROW** Parsley, fenugreek, rosewater, mint.

Exotic Mediterranean Rub
Makes about 115g (4oz)

This dry spice mix works best rubbed on lamb or chicken that's ready to grill.

4 tbsp sesame seeds
5 tbsp coriander seeds, crushed
2 tbsp ground fenugreek
2 tbsp dried oregano
1 tbsp ground cumin
1 tbsp kosher salt
Pinch of ground cinnamon

Toast the sesame seeds on the hob in a dry frying pan over a medium heat, shaking them frequently to avoid burning, until they are fragrant and just a shade darker (3–5 minutes). Combine all the ingredients in a small bowl and mix well. Stored in an airtight container in a cool, dark place, this dry rub will keep for a month.

Dill-Pomegranate Butter

GRILLED LAMB WITH ROCKET, BROAD BEANS, AND PORT-MUSTARD DRESSING

Marjoram is an underappreciated herb, with a more dynamic flavour than many of its better-known cousins. Here we use it with lamb, for which it has a particular affinity. The accompanying broad bean and rocket salad is a tribute to Chris's mom, who always served beans with her lamb chops. (If you have any dressing left over, don't throw it out — it's delicious drizzled over any kind of red meat, hot or cold.)

Serves 4 as a salad course or appetizer

THE SALAD

450g (1lb) boneless loin of lamb
4 tbsp olive oil
1 tsp finely chopped fresh garlic
2 tbsp roughly chopped fresh marjoram (or substitute oregano)
Kosher salt and freshly cracked black pepper
2 bunches rocket, trimmed, washed, and dried well
450g (1lb) fresh broad beans, podded and cooked, or 180g (6oz) frozen broad beans, cooked

THE DRESSING

1 tbsp Dijon mustard
1 tsp finely chopped shallots
2 tbsp port wine
5 tbsp extra virgin olive oil
Kosher salt and freshly cracked black pepper to taste

Build a multilevel fire in your grill (*see p31*). When the coals are all ignited, the flames have died down, and the temperature is hot (*see p34*), you're ready to cook.

Dry the lamb well with kitchen paper. Combine the oil, garlic, and marjoram in a small bowl, and mix well. Rub the lamb all over with this mixture, then sprinkle generously with salt and pepper. Place the lamb on the hot side of the grill and sear well (about 10 minutes per side). Move to the medium-hot area of the grill and continue to cook until the meat reaches the internal temperature you like (4–6 minutes per side for medium-rare). To check for doneness, insert a meat thermometer into the dead centre of the roast, let it sit for 5 seconds, then read the temperature: you're looking for 49°C (120°F) for rare, 52°C (126°F) for medium-rare (how we like it), 57°C (134°F) for medium, 66°C (150°F) for medium-well, and 70°C (160°F) for well-done. Remove the lamb from the grill, cover loosely with foil, and let it rest for 10 minutes.

While the lamb is resting, make the salad: combine the rocket and broad beans in a large bowl. In a small bowl, whisk together the mustard, shallots, and port; add the oil slowly in a thin stream, whisking until well-blended. Season with salt and pepper, then drizzle the beans and rocket with just enough dressing to coat lightly, and toss well. Divide among four salad plates.

Slice the lamb against the grain, 0.5–1cm (¼–½in) thick. Fan ¼ of the slices over each salad, drizzle with a little more dressing, and serve.

SIDES AND SNACKS

SO-CALLED "SIDE DISHES" CAN BE AS ENTICING
AND SATISYING AS ANY MAIN COURSE. AND IF
YOU'RE A VEGETARIAN, THIS IS THE CHAPTER FOR
YOU: PUT TWO OR THREE OF THESE DISHES
TOGETHER, AND YOU'VE GOT A GRILLED MEAL
THAT WILL HAVE YOU WONDERING WHERE
FLAMES HAVE BEEN ALL YOUR LIFE.

GRILL BREAD

We love grilled bread. Not only is it a great accompaniment to any meal, it also makes a wonderful appetizer when drizzled with some flavoured oil or dipped into a relish or salsa. Of course, you can always use store-bought bread, but it's more fun to make your own. Plus it always tastes better. Plus your guests are always impressed. This is a pretty standard flatbread recipe with some added beer for flavour and maize meal for texture, which makes it particularly good for the grill. When it comes off the coals, hot and slightly charred with its delightful crunch and its delicious yeasty taste, you'll be a hero.

Makes 4 flat loaves

THE INGREDIENTS

1 tbsp active dry yeast
350g (12oz) plain flour, divided
120ml (4fl oz) tepid water
2 tbsp olive oil, plus more for brushing

120ml (4fl oz) beer of your choice, at room temperature
4 tbsp maize meal, plus more for dusting
1 tsp kosher salt, plus more for sprinkling

Stir together the yeast and 60g (2oz) flour in the bowl of an electric mixer. Add the tepid water and mix until just blended. Cover with a damp towel and let stand in a warm, draught-free place (inside an airing cupboard, for example) for 30 minutes, until the mixture is thick and foamy and gives off a sound a bit like soda fizz when you stir it.

Add 2 tbsp of oil and the beer to the yeast mixture and mix well. Add the maize meal and 1 tsp salt, and begin adding the remaining 300g (10oz) of flour, about 4 tbsp at a time, to form a soft dough (you may not need all of the flour). Turn the dough out onto a floured board and knead, adding as much of the remaining flour as necessary to prevent the dough from sticking, until the dough is satiny and just slightly sticky (about 8 minutes).

Place the dough in an oiled bowl, turning once to coat. Cover loosely and let rise in a warm place until it has doubled in bulk (1–1½ hours). Divide the dough into quarters and form each piece into a ball. Sprinkle a baking tray with maize meal and put the balls of dough on the tray, then cover loosely and let rise again for 30 minutes. (At this point, you can cover the dough with cling film and refrigerate it until about an hour before you want to grill the bread.)

Build a fire in your grill. When the coals are all ignited, the flames have died down, and the temperature is medium (*see p34*), you're ready to cook.

Stretch each ball of dough into a rough circle or rectangle about 3mm (⅛in) thick and 25cm (10in) wide. Brush with additional olive oil and sprinkle with salt, then place it directly on the grill and cook until black spots form on the bottom and bubbles form on the top (about 4 minutes). Flip the bread over and grill the other side until golden and crusty (3–4 minutes more). Remove from the grill and serve immediately.

FLAVOURED OILS FOR GRILL BREAD

When your bread comes hot off the grill (*see previous page*), drizzle it with one of these oils and set it out along with the rest of the oil for dipping, and you've got a spectacular, slightly unusual appetizer. These oils will all keep for up to a week, covered and refrigerated. But since the oil will partially congeal when it's cold, remember to let it sit out to liquefy for about 15 minutes before serving.

ROAST GARLIC AND MARJORAM OIL

Makes about 180ml (6fl oz)

1 head garlic
120ml (4fl oz) extra virgin olive oil, divided
2 tsp kosher salt
1 tsp cracked black pepper
2 tbsp roughly chopped fresh marjoram
Kosher salt and freshly cracked black pepper to taste

Slice the top quarter off the head of garlic, put it in a bowl with 4 tbsp of the olive oil, salt, and pepper, and toss gently to combine. Wrap the garlic securely in 2 large sheets of heavy-duty foil.

Ash-roast or oven-roast the garlic: either place the parcel in the coals around the periphery of a fire, where the heat is less intense, or in an oven preheated to 150°C (300°F/Gas 2). Cook until the garlic feels soft when pressed through the foil (about 1 hour in the oven, or 30 minutes in the fire).

Remove the parcel from the fire or oven, cut the foil open, and wait until the garlic is cool enough to handle before squeezing the flesh from each clove.

Combine the garlic, the remaining olive oil, marjoram, and salt and pepper in a bowl and mix together well.

SPICY CUMIN AND ORANGE OIL

Makes about 180ml (6fl oz)

120ml (4fl oz) extra virgin olive oil
2 tbsp cumin seeds, freshly cracked
2 tbsp roughly chopped fresh oregano
1 tbsp finely chopped orange zest
1 tsp chilli pepper flakes
Kosher salt and freshly cracked black pepper to taste

Combine all the ingredients in a small saucepan and warm over a medium-low heat for 15 minutes. Let cool to room temperature before using.

SUN-DRIED TOMATO AND BASIL OIL

Makes about 240ml (8fl oz)

120ml (4fl oz) extra virgin olive oil
4 tbsp roughly chopped oil-packed sun-dried tomatoes
4 tbsp thinly sliced fresh basil leaves
1 tsp finely chopped fresh garlic
Kosher salt and freshly cracked black pepper to taste

Combine all the ingredients in a bowl and mix well. Allow to sit for at least 30 minutes before serving, so the tomatoes become lush and soft.

MEDITERRANEAN CHOPPED SALAD
ON GRILL BREAD

This chopped salad is a good accompaniment to a grilled meal all by itself. But arranged on top of rounds of home-grilled bread, it makes a substantial appetizer that works perfectly before a simple grilled seafood main course. It's also a very satisfying light lunch on a hot day, along with a glass of rosé and a rich dessert like grilled banana upside-down cake (*see p322*). If you want to make it easy on yourself, buy pitted olives for this one.

Serves 4–8 as an appetizer

THE INGREDIENTS

1 recipe Grill Bread (*see p270*), shaped into 4 rounds
  but not cooked
3 tbsp extra virgin olive oil
2 tomatoes, about the size of tennis balls, cored,
  deseeded, and diced small
2 cucumbers, halved, deseeded, and diced small
175g (6oz) brine-cured black olives, such as
  kalamata, pitted and roughly chopped
20g (¾oz) roughly chopped fresh parsley
5 tbsp extra virgin olive oil
4 tbsp red wine vinegar
60g (2oz) crumbled feta cheese
Kosher salt and freshly cracked black pepper to taste

Build a fire in your grill. When the coals are all ignited, the flames have died down, and the temperature is medium (*see p34*), you're ready to cook.

Brush the bread rounds with oil on both sides, then place on the grill directly over the coals and cook until nicely toasted and brown on one side (about 4 minutes). Flip the bread over and grill the other side until golden and crusty (3–4 minutes more).

While the bread is on the grill, combine the tomatoes, cucumbers, olives, and parsley in a bowl. Whisk together the oil and vinegar in another bowl, then add just enough dressing to moisten the salad, tossing gently until evenly mixed.

Place a grilled bread round on each salad plate. At the last minute, toss the feta cheese with the tomato salad and season with salt and pepper. Top each bread round with a portion of the salad and serve.

TZATZIKI DIP FOR GRILL BREAD

This Greek-style mixture is a wonderful dipping sauce for grilled bread. For the best flavour and texture, use Greek-style whole-milk yogurt. If you want to be a bit more formal, you can also serve this as a sit-down appetizer, with the cucumber mixture spooned generously over the rounds of bread.

Serves 4 as an appetizer

THE INGREDIENTS

1 recipe Grill Bread (*see p270*), shaped into 4 rounds
  but not cooked
3 tbsp extra virgin olive oil
½ cucumber, peeled if desired, diced small
115g (4oz) plain yogurt
3 tbsp roughly chopped fresh mint
1 tbsp fresh lemon juice
1 tbsp ground cumin
Kosher salt and freshly cracked black pepper to taste

Build a fire in your grill. When the coals are all ignited, the flames have died down, and the temperature is medium (*see p34*), you're ready to cook.

Brush the bread rounds with oil on both sides, then place on the grill directly over the coals and cook until nicely toasted and brown on one side (about 4 minutes). Flip the bread over and grill the other side until golden and crusty (3–4 minutes more).

While the bread is on the grill, combine the cucumber, yogurt, mint, lemon juice, cumin, and salt and pepper in a bowl and mix well.

Cut the bread into wedges or just set it out so people can tear a piece off and spoon the tzatziki on top.

BLUE CHEESE, PEAR, AND CARAMELISED ONION PIZZAS

Putting a foil tray over food on the grill creates a sort of mini-oven. It's a useful strategy for cooking thick cuts of meat all the way through without burning them on the outside. Here we use this approach to melt blue cheese on grill bread without putting it over a fire so hot that it would burn the dough on the bottom.

Serves 4–6 as an appetizer

THE INGREDIENTS

6 tbsp extra virgin olive oil, divided

3 red onions, peeled and sliced into thin rings

Kosher salt and freshly cracked black pepper to taste

1 recipe Grill Bread (*see p270*), shaped into 4 rounds but not cooked

2 ripe but firm pears, cored and sliced thin

60g (2oz) crumbled blue cheese of your choice

4 tbsp roughly chopped fresh parsley

On the hob, heat 3 tablespoons of the extra virgin olive oil in a large sauté pan or frying pan over a medium heat until it is hot but not smoking. Add the onions, sprinkle with salt and pepper, and sauté, stirring occasionally, until the onions start to soften (about 5 minutes). Reduce the heat to low and continue to cook, stirring often, until the onions are well caramelised (20–30 minutes).

While the onions are cooking, build a fire in your grill. When the coals are all ignited, the flames have died down, and the temperature is medium (*see p34*), you're ready to cook.

When the onions are ready, brush the bread rounds on both sides with the remaining 3 tbsp oil, then place on the grill directly over the coals and cook until nicely toasted and brown on one side (about 4 minutes). Flip the bread over and top each round with a pile of caramelized onions, then arrange the pear slices over the onions and scatter the blue cheese on top. Invert a foil tray over the pizzas and continue to cook until the cheese starts to melt (3–4 minutes more).

Cut the pizzas into wedges with a large, sharp knife, arrange on a serving plate, sprinkle with parsley, and serve.

PEACH, PARMESAN, AND CRISP PARMA HAM PIZZAS

Fruit on grill bread might seem like an odd idea, but this combination of sweet, lush peaches, nutty Parmesan, and rich, salty Parma ham will win you over. Be careful not to leave the ham over the coals too long; you don't need to cook it, you just want to crisp it up and give it a little smokiness.

Serves 4–6 as an appetizer

THE INGREDIENTS

175g (6oz) very thinly sliced Parma ham
4 tbsp extra virgin olive oil
1 tsp finely chopped fresh garlic
1 recipe Grill Bread (*see p270*), shaped into 4 rounds
   but not cooked
2 ripe but firm peaches, halved, stoned, and sliced
   thinly
4 tbsp freshly grated Parmesan cheese
2 tbsp roughly chopped fresh basil

Build a fire in your grill. When the coals are all ignited, the flames have died down, and the temperature is medium (*see p34*), you're ready to cook.

Put the Parma ham slices on the grill directly over the coals and cook until just crisp (about 1 minute). Set aside.

Combine the olive oil and garlic in a small bowl and mix well. Brush the bread rounds on both sides with garlic oil, then place on the grill directly over the coals and cook until nicely toasted and brown on one side (about 4 minutes). Flip the bread over and arrange the grilled ham and some of the peach slices on each one. Season lightly with salt and pepper and scatter the cheese on top, then invert a foil tray over the pizzas and continue to cook until the cheese starts to melt (3–4 minutes more).

Cut the pizzas into wedges with a large, sharp knife, drizzle with some of the remaining garlic oil, then arrange on a serving plate, sprinkle with basil, and serve.

GRILLED PRAWN, BACON, AND CHEESE PIZZAS

We figure that almost any combination we like in general, we'll also like on top of our grill bread. Since we love prawns, bacon, and cheese – I mean, really, who doesn't? – we decided to give it a try. It turned out to be one of our top favourite pizza choices, and everyone else we've tried it out on has been equally enthusiastic.

Serves 4–6 as an appetizer

THE INGREDIENTS

12 raw prawns, 16/20 size, peeled and halved
   lengthways
6 streaky bacon rashers, diced small
4 tbsp extra virgin olive oil, divided
2 tbsp roughly chopped fresh thyme
Kosher salt and freshly cracked black pepper to taste
1 recipe Grill Bread (*see p270*), shaped into 4 rounds
   but not cooked
1 cup grated Asiago or other hard Italian cheese, such
   as Parmigiano Reggiano

On the hob, cook the bacon in a sauté pan over a medium heat until crisp (6–8 minutes). Drain well.

Build a fire in your grill. When the coals are all ignited, the flames have died down, and the temperature is medium (*see p34*), you're ready to cook.

Combine the prawns, bacon, 1 tbsp of the olive oil, thyme, and salt and pepper in a bowl and mix until the prawns and bacon are evenly coated.

Brush the bread rounds on both sides with the remaining 3 tbsp of olive oil, then place them on the grill directly over the coals and cook until nicely toasted and brown on one side (about 4 minutes). Flip the bread over and top each round with some of the prawn mixture, then scatter the cheese on top. Invert a foil tray over the pizzas, and continue to cook until the prawns are just cooked through and the cheese is starting to melt (3–4 minutes more).

Cut the pizzas into wedges with a large, sharp knife. Arrange on a serving plate, and serve.

GRILLED NEW POTATOES WITH ROSEMARY, GARLIC, AND BLACK OLIVES

We're strongly in favour of anything that puts a nice, brown crust on a potato. Here we use live fire to do it, which also gives the potatoes a lovely slightly smoky taste. Before the potatoes go on the grill, we parboil them (to ensure they cook all the way through over the fire), then when they come off the grill, we coat them with Italian flavourings.

Serves 4 as a side dish

THE INGREDIENTS

20 small new potatoes (or 10 larger ones, halved), well-washed

3 tbsp vegetable oil

2 tbsp finely chopped garlic

Kosher salt and freshly cracked black pepper to taste

60g (2oz) roughly chopped pitted kalamata or other brine-cured black olives

4 tbsp extra virgin olive oil

Juice of 1 lemon (about 4 tbsp)

2 tbsp roughly chopped fresh rosemary

Kosher salt and freshly cracked black pepper to taste

On the hob, bring a pan of salted water to the boil and cook the potatoes, uncovered, just until they can be pierced easily with a fork but still offer some resistance (6–8 minutes). Immediately plunge them into ice water to stop the cooking, drain well, and refrigerate until cold.

Build a fire in your grill. When the coals are all ignited, the flames have died down, and the temperature is medium (*see p34*), you're ready to cook.

Put the chilled potatoes in a large bowl. Add the vegetable oil, garlic, and salt and pepper and toss gently until the potatoes are evenly coated. Thread the potatoes onto skewers; if they are halved, put each half facing the same way so that the cut sides lie flat. Arrange the skewers on the grill over the coals and cook until the potatoes are golden-brown (3–4 minutes). Flip over and cook for 2 minutes more.

When the potatoes are done, carefully push them off the skewers back into the same large bowl. Add the olives, olive oil, lemon juice, rosemary, and salt and pepper to taste, and toss gently until the potatoes are evenly coated. Transfer to a serving dish and serve immediately.

BALSAMIC RED ONIONS
WITH BASIL AND PARMESAN

This easy side dish is ideal for anyone who loves Italian flavours and grilled onions – and that's a very wide group indeed. Add that to the fact that it takes next to no time to prepare, and you have a dish with nearly universal appeal. Cut the onion rings nice and thick, and they'll be less likely to fall apart on the grill.

Serves 4–6 as a side dish

THE INGREDIENTS

2 large red onions, peeled and sliced into rings about
   2.5cm (1in) thick
2 tbsp vegetable oil
Kosher salt and freshly cracked black pepper
4 tbsp extra virgin olive oil
4 tbsp balsamic vinegar
15g (½oz) thinly sliced fresh basil leaves
4 tbsp grated parmesan cheese

Build a fire in your grill. When the coals are all ignited, the flames have died down, and the temperature is medium (*see p34*), you're ready to cook.

Rub the onion slices with the vegetable oil, keeping the rings together. Sprinkle the onions generously with salt and pepper. Put them on the grill directly over the coals and cook until soft and golden-brown – about 10 minutes per side.

When the onions are done, transfer them to a medium bowl and add the olive oil, vinegar, basil, and parmesan, tossing to separate the onion slices into rings and incorporate all of the ingredients.

Pile the grilled onions on a serving plate and drizzle generously with the remaining dressing.

MORE SIMPLE GRILLED VEGETABLES

With your fire temperature at medium (*see p34*), you can treat your guests to a tasty selection of grilled vegetables. The red peppers below would team perfectly with the grilled onions opposite (*see also overleaf*) to accompany any Mediterranean-style main dish – or, if your meal has more of an Asian flavour, try the aubergine and courgette recipes. Each serves 4–6 people as a side dish.

GRILLED RED PEPPERS WITH PINE NUTS AND PARSLEY

5 red peppers, halved, cored, and seeded
4 tbsp olive or vegetable oil
Kosher salt and freshly cracked black pepper
1 recipe Parsley-Pine Nut Relish (*see p262*)

Rub the pepper halves lightly with oil and sprinkle them generously with salt and pepper, then put them on the grill directly over the coals and cook until they are golden-brown but still crisp (2–3 minutes per side). When the peppers are done, cut them into thin strips and transfer them to a large bowl. Add the relish to the peppers and toss until evenly mixed. Pile the peppers on a serving plate and serve immediately.

GRILLED AUBERGINE WITH GINGER-SOY BARBECUE SAUCE

1 large aubergine, cut into slices about 2.5cm (1in) thick
3 tbsp olive oil
Kosher salt and freshly cracked black pepper
1 recipe Ginger-Soy Barbecue Sauce (*see p228*)

Rub the aubergine slices on both sides with the oil and sprinkle generously with salt and pepper, then put them on the grill directly over the coals and cook, turning once, until the interior is tender and moist all the way through (3–4 minutes per side). Brush with the barbecue sauce during the last 30 seconds of cooking on each side. Transfer the aubergine slices to a serving plate and serve, passing the remaining barbecue sauce on the side.

ASIAN-STYLE GRILLED COURGETTES

4 medium courgettes, halved lengthways to make 8 planks about 2.5cm (1in) thick
1 recipe Sesame-Ginger Paste (*see p231*)
Kosher salt

Rub the courgette planks generously with the sesame paste and sprinkle them lightly with salt, then put them on the grill and cook, turning once, until the courgettes look moist all the way through and the interior has lost its raw, opaque look (3–4 minutes per side). Transfer the courgettes to a serving plate and serve.

SWEETCORN ON THE GRILL

There's nothing better than fresh sweetcorn on the grill. Because it's so popular, people have developed many ways of cooking it. We provide three here: they all make sense to us, because each has its own virtues. Whichever method you choose to use, our Latin Flavour Modifiers (*see overleaf*) are the perfect accompaniment to the end result.

Allow 1 ear of sweetcorn per person

FIRST METHOD: HUSK-ON AND SOAKED

This is a good method to use if you are a big fan of tenderness in your corn, but aren't too concerned with time.

Soak the ears in water for 15 minutes.

Place the ears on the grill over a medium fire (*see p34*) and let them steam until they are just cooked through (about 15–20 minutes). To check for doneness, peel back the husk on one ear and poke the kernels to be sure they are tender.

Remove the husks and silks, brush on a little butter, season with salt and pepper, then roll the ears around on the grill ever so slightly to add a little char.

SECOND METHOD: NAKED CORN

This is a good everyday approach to grilling corn: it's easy, it's quick, and you get good corn flavour plus a nice smokiness.

Strip the husks and silks from the ears.

Place the ears over a medium-low fire (*see p34*) and let them cook for 3–5 minutes, rolling them around for even cooking, until they are just golden-brown. To check for doneness, poke the kernels to be sure they are tender.

THIRD METHOD: ASH-ROASTED

This is probably our favourite approach — not only does it produce very smoky-flavoured corn, but it also allows you to cook it with some of the butter, salt, and pepper already on it.

Strip the husks and silks from the ears.

Wrap each ear, along with butter, salt, and pepper to your taste, in a double layer of foil. Put the parcels in the coals of your grill fire for 12–15 minutes. To check for doneness, peel open one of the parcels and poke at the kernels to be sure they are tender.

Remove the ears from the foil parcels, brush on more butter, season with more salt and pepper to taste, and serve.

LATIN FLAVOUR MODIFIERS FOR SWEETCORN

These bursts of flavour with a citrus twist are particularly welcome at the height of sweetcorn season, when you want grilled corn (*see pp288–9*) with every meal but are looking for a little variety in how you serve it. Each of these should be enough for a dozen or more ears.

ORANGE-CHIPOTLE BUTTER

120ml (4fl oz) orange juice
2 tbsp finely chopped chipotle peppers in adobo sauce
115g (4oz) unsalted butter, softened

On the hob, bring the orange juice to the boil in a small saucepan over a high heat. Reduce the heat to medium-low and simmer vigorously until reduced by two-thirds in volume (15–20 minutes). Remove the pan from the heat, stir in the chipotles, and let cool to room temperature. When cooled, add to the butter and mash it all together well. Top each ear of hot grilled sweetcorn with a generous helping of the butter. (Any leftover butter can be wrapped in greaseproof paper and refrigerated; it will keep for up to 3 days.)

CUMIN SALT WITH LIME

115g (4oz) kosher salt
4 tbsp cumin seeds
3 limes, cut into wedges

Combine the salt and cumin seeds in a small sauté pan over a low heat. Cook, stirring constantly, until the seeds start to smoke slightly and become fragrant (2–3 minutes). Set aside. Squeeze the lime wedges over the grilled sweetcorn, then sprinkle liberally with the flavoured salt.

CORIANDER-LIME BUTTER

4 tbsp roughly chopped fresh coriander
Juice of 1 lime (about 2 tbsp)
1 tbsp chilli powder
115g (4oz) unsalted butter, softened

Work the coriander, lime juice, and chilli powder into the butter in a small bowl, mixing well. You can use the butter right away, or wrap it in cling film, shape it into a square log, and refrigerate until firm.

When you're ready to serve the sweetcorn, place the butter, unwrapped, in a shallow dish. Let your guests roll their own corn on the butter (the way most people do at home when they eat corn on the cob and no one's watching).

MALAYSIA: FOOD FANTASY

To put it mildly, we were not thrilled to be stranded overnight in the gritty truck-stop town of Johor Bahru, Malaysia. But, figuring we might as well make the best of it, we decided to check out the local open-air market.

The moment we walked in, our overnight stay began to seem less a delay than a delight. We wandered past stalls featuring frogs' legs, boar snouts, and huge piles of greens whose names we didn't know, then browsed the seafood section, where giant eels, cockles, spiny lobsters, and four types of crabs lay on glistening rows of ice. Next we hit the fruit stands, crowded with specimens that seemed too bizarre to be real: red-orange rambutans, bristling with pointy spikes; purple-brown mangosteens, the white inner flesh tasting of molasses, lemon, and cream; beadlike chiku, gooey and sweet as boiled icing; huge orange-yellow jackfruit, mealy and mellow, hinting of vanilla. Other fruits, like mango and papaya, were familiar in form, but had flavours of a depth and complexity we had never experienced. When we walked back to the hotel at dusk, we discovered that the car park had been transformed into a hawker centre, with dozens of bicycle-propelled food stands arranged around a handful of folding tables and chairs. Excited, we joined the crowd and sampled dish after dish – stingray tail dabbed with hot sauce, wrapped in a banana leaf, and roasted in hot coals; plump and satisfyingly fatty curried frogs' legs; water greens sautéed with chillies and garlic. Instead of dessert, we ordered what looked like a fruit salad, rich with the variety we had seen earlier at the market. It was a classic example of Malay food, the sweet, fecund intensity of the fruits perfectly complemented by a peanut sauce laced with chillies and a hint of *belacan*, their beloved fermented shrimp paste. The moral, it seemed, was clear: never underestimate a truck stop.

SPICY FRUIT SALAD
WITH LIME-PEANUT DRESSING

Inspired by Malaysian *rojak*, this is a fruit salad with a bit of savoury/spicy attitude. If you want to make this more authentic and have access to (and a taste for) the shrimp paste called *belacan*, add a teaspoonful or so to the dressing. Although native to the Americas, the jicama is very popular in Asian cuisines. It's sometimes called the Mexican potato, which does little justice to its juicy crispness and sweet taste. If you can't find jicama, use a crisp green apple or Asian pear instead.

Serves 4 as a side dish

1 mango, stoned, peeled, and diced medium
1 papaya, deseeded, peeled, and diced medium
60g (2oz) pineapple, diced medium
60g (2oz) jicama (or substitute apple), diced medium
4 tbsp roughly chopped fresh coriander

For the dressing:
4 tbsp roughly chopped roasted unsalted peanuts
1 tbsp finely chopped fresh ginger
1 tbsp finely chopped red or green fresh chilli pepper of your choice
Juice of 2 limes (about 4 tbsp)
2 tbsp soy sauce
1 tbsp soft dark brown sugar

Combine all the fruits and the coriander in a large bowl.

Combine all the dressing ingredients in a small bowl and whisk until well-blended.

Add just enough of the dressing to the fruit mixture to moisten, toss gently, and serve.

CHILLI-GRILLED SUMMER SQUASH

We like the mild flavour of summer squash, but lots of our friends complain that it's a little boring. Well, this one is for them. The paste that we coat the squash planks with during the last minute of cooking is hot and intense with dried chillies and other deep flavours. Pass a bowl of it around separately when you serve this, in case your daredevil friends want more.

Serves 4–6 as a side dish

THE SQUASH

4 medium summer squash, unpeeled,
  halved lengthways to make 8 planks
  about 2.5cm (1in) thick

2 tbsp olive oil
Kosher salt and freshly cracked black pepper

THE CHILLI PASTE

4 tbsp crushed ancho chillies or other dried chillies
  of your choice
4 tbsp roughly chopped fresh coriander
4 tbsp olive oil
2 tbsp cumin seeds
Juice of 1 lime (about 2 tbsp)
1 tbsp finely chopped fresh garlic
1 tbsp kosher salt
1 tbsp freshly cracked black pepper

Build a fire in your grill. When the coals are all ignited, the flames have died down, and the temperature is medium (*see p34*), you're ready to cook.

Combine all the chilli paste ingredients in a small bowl, mix well, and set aside.

Rub the squash planks lightly on both sides with oil and sprinkle them generously with salt and pepper, then put them on the grill directly over the coals and cook, turning once, until the interior is moist all the way through and has lost its raw, opaque look (3–4 minutes per side). Brush them with the chilli paste during the last minute of cooking.

Arrange the squash planks on a serving plate and serve warm or at room temperature. Pass the remaining chilli paste separately so that fire-eaters can add more.

GRILLED BROCCOLI WITH LEMON BUTTER

We are big fans of broccoli, so we're always looking for new ways to cook it. This rather novel approach – dividing the head into quarters, blanching it, then giving it a nice gentle char on the grill before mixing it with butter and lemon juice – adds an appealing smoky dimension to an old favourite.

Serves 4 as a side dish

THE INGREDIENTS

1 large head broccoli, sliced lengthways into
    quarters
Kosher salt and freshly cracked black pepper
3 tbsp olive oil
115g (4oz) unsalted butter, softened
Juice of ½ lemon (about 2 tbsp)

Build a fire in your grill. When the coals are all ignited, the flames have died down, and the temperature is medium (*see p34*), you're ready to cook.

While you wait for the fire to reach cooking temperature, on the hob, bring a pan of salted water to the boil. Blanch the broccoli quarters for 1 minute, then drain well.

Put the blanched broccoli in a large bowl, sprinkle it generously with salt and pepper, drizzle it with the oil, and toss to coat. Put the broccoli on the grill directly over the coals and cook until tender (2–3 minutes per side), then return to the same large bowl.

Add the butter, lemon juice, and more salt and pepper to taste to the hot broccoli, tossing gently to coat. Transfer to a serving dish and serve immediately.

GRILLED POTATO STEAKS
WITH BACON AND SOURED CREAM

Who doesn't love a baked potato with the works – butter, soured cream, bacon, and chives? Here we go that classic combo one better by slicing the potatoes into thick planks, which we like to call "steaks", then grilling them before piling on the extras. This is the side dish to make when you're having a grilled steak dinner.

Serves 4

THE INGREDIENTS

2 large baking potatoes, well-scrubbed (not peeled)
4 rashers bacon, diced small
2 tbsp olive oil
Kosher salt and freshly cracked black pepper to taste
142ml (5fl oz) soured cream
1 small bunch chives, finely chopped
60g (2oz) unsalted butter (optional)

Build a fire in your grill. When the coals are all ignited, the flames have died down, and the temperature is medium (*see p34*), you're ready to cook.

While you wait for the fire, cut thin slices lengthways off 2 parallel sides of each potato so you can lay them flat. Now cut each potato in half lengthways to make 2 steaks, each about 3cm (1–1½in) thick.

On the hob, bring a large pan of boiling salted water to the boil and reduce the heat to a gentle simmer. Cook the potatoes gently in the simmering water until just done but still very firm (8–9 minutes). To check for doneness, poke with a toothpick: It should slide into the potato, but meet with a fair amount of resistance. Drain the potatoes and pat them dry with kitchen paper.

Meanwhile, cook the bacon in a small sauté pan or frying pan over a medium heat until crisp (6–8 minutes), then transfer to kitchen paper to drain.

Brush the potato steaks with oil and sprinkle them generously with salt and pepper, then put them on the grill directly over the coals and cook, turning once, until they are really crisp and brown (4–5 minutes per side).

Arrange the potatoes on a serving plate and top with the bacon, soured cream, and chives, plus butter if using.

ASIAN GRILLED COURGETTES

Gardeners often complain about having a glut of courgettes, but we love them. They're a supremely adaptable vegetable, easily paired with all kinds of flavour footprints, like the Southeast Asian sauce we brush on them in this dish. Cutting the courgettes into planks makes it easy to grill them to tenderness without burning the outside.

Serves 4 as a side dish

THE INGREDIENTS

4 medium courgettes, unpeeled, halved lengthways to
   make 8 planks about 2.5cm (1in) thick
2 tbsp sesame oil
Kosher salt and freshly cracked white pepper to taste
   (or substitute black pepper)
1 recipe Mango-Chilli Sauce (*see p210*)

Build a fire in your grill. When the coals are all ignited, the flames have died down, and the temperature is medium (*see p34*), you're ready to cook.

Rub the courgette planks lightly on both sides with sesame oil and sprinkle them generously with salt and pepper, then put them on the grill directly over the coals and cook, turning once, until the interior is moist all the way through and has lost its raw, opaque look (3–4 minutes per side).

Add the grilled courgettes to the bowl of sauce and toss gently to coat. Transfer to a serving plate and serve warm or at room temperature.

AUBERGINE AND TOMATO HOBO PACK

If you want to make delicious, slightly unusual side dishes without a lot of work, hobo packs (*see p19*) are for you. Just assemble the foil package, slide it into the coals, and let it cook while you make the rest of the meal on top of the grill grid. This combination of aubergine and tomatoes is a classic pairing found throughout the Mediterranean world, and for good reason — the rich aubergine and sweet-tart tomato complement each other perfectly. Add garlic, onion, oregano, and hot pepper, and you've got a super-tasty side dish that goes with just about any meal. It's also a delicious vegetarian main course for two.

Serves 4 as a side dish

THE INGREDIENTS

2 small aubergines, unpeeled, cut into 5cm (2in) cubes

2 tomatoes about the size of tennis balls, cored and diced large

1 red onion, peeled and diced large

5 peeled garlic cloves

5 tbsp extra virgin olive oil

2 tbsp roughly chopped fresh oregano

1 tsp chilli pepper flakes

Kosher salt and freshly cracked black pepper to taste

Combine all the ingredients in a large bowl and toss gently until evenly mixed.

Tear off 4 sheets of heavy-duty foil, each about 60cm (24in) long, and stack them one on top of the other. Arrange the vegetables in the centre of the top sheet.

Fold up the sheets around the ingredients, one after another, turning the package one-quarter turn between each sheet and making sure that each sheet is well-sealed around the food. If necessary, divide the ingredients in half and make 2 hobo packs. Or, place the ingredients in a deep disposable foil tray (*see overleaf*) and cover tightly with a double layer of heavy-duty foil.

Place the hobo pack (or packs) in the coals around the periphery of the fire, where the heat is less intense. Pile the coals up around the pack and cook until the aubergine is cooked through (20–30 minutes).

Remove the pack from the coals and unwrap the foil; if the vegetables need more time, put the pack back in the coals or in a 150°C (300°F/Gas 2) oven until it's done.

MORE HOBO PACK COMBINATIONS

All kinds of vegetables and fruits can be cooked using the hobo pack method. It's a great way to cook sweetcorn, for example (*see p288*) — and we also use it for some fantastic desserts (*see pp318–9*). You can cook individual vegetables with just a little butter or olive oil, salt, and pepper, or experiment with combinations — the approach we prefer. Here's a quartet of our favourites. For each, follow exactly the same method as on the page opposite. Each recipe serves 4 as a side dish.

NEW POTATOES AND GARLIC

Potatoes, garlic, and onion form one of those combinations of ingredients that makes your mouth water any time you smell it cooking. It's even better when it has a little edge of smoke from cooking in the coals. This is a wonderful side dish with a big, juicy grilled steak.

16 new potatoes about the size of golf balls, scrubbed but not peeled

1 red onion, peeled and diced large

1 large head garlic, separated into cloves and peeled

4 tbsp olive oil

Kosher salt and freshly cracked black pepper to taste

MUSHROOM AND PICKLING ONION

Combined with mushrooms, butter, parsley, and a dash of sherry, these small, sweet onions make a delicious and versatile side dish. If you feel like laying out a little more cash, wild mushrooms take this dish to an even higher level.

450g (1lb) white mushrooms, stems trimmed

12 pickling onions about the size of golf balls, finely chopped

115g (4oz) chilled unsalted butter, diced

4 tbsp roughly chopped fresh parsley

2 tbsp dry sherry

Kosher salt and freshly cracked black pepper to taste

SWEET POTATO AND GREEN GRAPE

When you unwrap the foil from this combo, the rich, moist sweet potatoes flavoured with smoke, sage, and brown sugar and complemented by the sweetness of the grapes will be a revelation.

2 sweet potatoes, peeled and diced large

200g (7oz) green grapes

Juice of 1 lemon (about 4 tbsp)

4 tbsp extra virgin olive oil

9 roughly chopped fresh sage leaves

1 tbsp soft dark brown sugar

Kosher salt and freshly cracked black pepper to taste

POTATO AND LEEK

Vichyssoise may be the most well-known pairing of potatoes and leeks, but they are also wonderful together in this simple but rather elegant hobo pack. Make sure that you wash the leeks well; the best approach is to cut them in half lengthways and then immerse them for several minutes in a sinkful of cold water. After that, rinse them a couple more times in cold running water.

2 large baking potatoes, scrubbed well and diced large

4 medium leeks, white parts only, trimmed, very well-washed, and sliced thin

30g (1oz) roughly chopped spring onions, with green tops

115g (4oz) chilled unsalted butter, diced

Kosher salt and freshly cracked black pepper to taste

GLAZED SWEET POTATOES

Sweet potatoes have a wonderful earthy sweetness that is beautifully enhanced by a little char from the grill. Glazed with a simple maple syrup-butter combination, they are a fantastic side dish for just about any grilled meal, particularly in early autumn. We are especially fond of them with the grilled veal chops on p56, or the pheasant breasts on p170.

Serves 4 as a side dish

THE INGREDIENTS

3 sweet potatoes, peeled and cut diagonally into slices
   about 2.5cm (1in) thick
5 tbsp maple syrup
75g (2½oz) unsalted butter
2 tbsp olive oil
Kosher salt and freshly cracked black pepper

Build a fire in your grill. When the coals are all ignited, the flames have died down, and the temperature is medium (*see p34*), you're ready to cook.

On the hob, bring a large pan of boiling salted water to the boil and reduce the heat to a gentle simmer. Cook the sweet potato slices gently in the simmering water until just tender but still very firm (6–8 minutes). To check for doneness, poke one of the slices with a toothpick: it should slide in, but still meet with a fair amount of resistance. Drain the slices and pat them dry with kitchen paper.

Combine the maple syrup and butter in a small saucepan over a medium heat, stirring occasionally, until the butter melts. Remove from the heat and set aside.

Brush the sweet potatoes with oil and sprinkle them generously with salt and pepper, then put them on the grill directly over the coals and cook, turning once, until they are nicely browned and tender (3–4 minutes per side). Brush the slices with the syrup mixture during the last minute of cooking on each side. Serve hot or at room temperature, drizzled with a bit more of the syrup mixture.

GRILLED MUSHROOMS
WITH BACON AND PARMESAN

Oh, yeah, oh, yeah. This is one of the great side dishes of the grilled repertoire. It's rich, it's earthy, it's cheesy and crisp and a little bit hot, and it's just plain delicious. Your friends will be asking you to make this one every time they come over, no matter what else is on the menu.

Serves 4 as a side dish

THE INGREDIENTS

115g (4oz) streaky bacon, diced small
675g (1½lb) white mushrooms, stems trimmed
4 tbsp olive oil
1 tbsp finely chopped fresh garlic
1 tsp chilli pepper flakes
Kosher salt and freshly cracked black pepper to taste
4 tbsp grated parmesan cheese
4 tbsp roughly chopped fresh parsley
30g (1oz) unsalted butter, softened

On the hob cook the bacon until crisp in a sauté pan over a medium heat (6–8 minutes). Drain well and set aside.

Build a fire in your grill. When the coals are all ignited, the flames have died down, and the temperature is medium (*see p34*), you're ready to cook.

Combine the mushrooms, olive oil, garlic, chilli flakes, and salt and pepper in a bowl and toss until evenly coated. If the mushrooms are small, thread them onto skewers. Put the mushrooms on the grill directly over the coals and cook until they are moist all the way through – about 10 minutes. Put the mushrooms into a large bowl and immediately add the bacon, parmesan, parsley, and butter, tossing gently until the mushrooms are evenly coated with butter and cheese. If necessary, season with more salt and pepper to taste, and serve immediately.

GRILLED PORTOBELLO MUSHROOMS
WITH BUTTER AND GARLIC

Portobello mushrooms should be a staple of every griller's repertoire. Large enough so they are easy to handle on the grill, full of that deep, rich, earthy flavour that we love in mushrooms, and these days very widely available, they are a great option for a quick but elegant side dish. Just sear them on the grill, toss them with a little butter, garlic, and parsley, and you're there.

Serves 4–6 as a side dish

THE INGREDIENTS

6 Portobello mushrooms, as large as you can find
    (about 900g (2lb) in total), stems removed
3 tbsp olive oil
Kosher salt and freshly cracked black pepper
85g (3oz) unsalted butter, at room temperature
1 tbsp finely chopped fresh garlic
4 tbsp roughly chopped fresh parsley

Build a fire in your grill. When the coals are all ignited, the flames have died down, and the temperature is medium (*see p34*), you're ready to cook.

Rub the mushrooms with oil and sprinkle them generously with salt and pepper, then put them on the grill directly over the coals and cook until they are tender and slightly seared (6–8 minutes per side). If you want to check for doneness, cut into one of the mushrooms to be sure it is moist all the way through, rather than dry at the centre.

As soon as the mushrooms are done, cut them into thick slices and place them in a bowl. Top the hot mushrooms with the butter and garlic, tossing gently to coat them all over. Transfer to a serving dish, garnish with parsley, and serve immediately.

GRILLED SHIITAKE MUSHROOMS
WITH SPRING ONIONS AND GINGER

Like Portobellos (*see facing page*), shiitake mushrooms seem made for the grill. As with most foods, we think they're best teamed with flavours from their region of origin, so here we toss them with a simple Asian-style dressing right as they come off the grill; that way, they absorb the flavours quickly.

Serves 4–6 as a side dish

THE MUSHROOMS

900g (2lb) large fresh shiitake mushrooms, tough bottom part of stems trimmed off

Kosher salt and freshly cracked black pepper

1 tbsp sesame oil

1 tbsp vegetable oil

THE DRESSING

3 tbsp soy sauce

2 tbsp dry sherry

1 tbsp sesame oil

1 tbsp peeled and finely chopped fresh ginger

THE GARNISH

2 tbsp thinly sliced spring onions, white and light green parts

Build a fire in your grill. When the coals are all ignited, the flames have died down, and the temperature is medium-hot (*see p34*), you're ready to cook.

Combine the dressing ingredients in a small bowl, mix well, and set aside.

Place the mushrooms in a large bowl, sprinkle generously with salt and pepper, and drizzle with the sesame and vegetable oils, tossing to coat. Put them on the grill directly over the coals and cook until they are browned and crisp and have grill marks on them (3–4 minutes per side). If you want to check for doneness, cut into one of the mushrooms to be sure it is moist all the way through, rather than dry at the centre.

When the mushrooms are done, return them to the bowl you originally tossed them in, add the dressing, and toss gently to coat. Transfer the mushrooms to a serving dish, garnish with the spring onions, and serve.

BUFFALO ASPARAGUS

Asparagus, quite delicious grilled all by itself, is also a very adaptable vegetable, compatible with a wide range of flavourings that actually bring out, rather than mask, its subtle but distinctive taste. Okay, so you might think that the "buffalo" approach, with the intensity of hot sauce and blue cheese, is going too far — but you would be wrong. Somehow these flavours all work together, and this is one of the most popular side dishes we've come up with recently. It also makes an excellent appetizer.

Serves 4 as a side dish

THE INGREDIENTS

24 asparagus spears, slightly larger in diameter than
    a pencil, trimmed
2 tbsp olive oil
Kosher salt and freshly cracked black pepper
4 tbsp of your favourite hot sauce
45g (1½oz) soft butter
60g (2oz) blue cheese

Build a fire in your grill. When the coals are all ignited, the flames have died down, and the temperature is medium (*see p34*), you're ready to cook.

Rub the asparagus with oil and sprinkle generously with salt and pepper, then put on the grill directly over the coals (you can use skewers to keep them together if you wish). Cook until the spears are browned and tender (4–6 minutes).

Combine the hot sauce and butter in a large bowl, mashing until smooth. Add the asparagus and toss gently to coat with the sauce.

Arrange the asparagus on a serving plate, crumble the blue cheese over the top, and serve.

SIPS AND SWEETS

TO DO YOUR BEST WORK AT THE GRILL, IT HELPS TO HAVE A FAVOURITE BEVERAGE CLOSE AT HAND. AND OF COURSE, YOU'LL WANT TO PROVIDE SOME FOR YOUR GUESTS, TOO. SO HERE THEY ARE, ALONG WITH A HANDFUL OF SWEET ENDINGS TO COMPLETE THE MEAL. NEVER THOUGHT OF DOING DESSERTS ON THE GRILL? THINK AGAIN.

GRILLED MANGOES WITH ICE CREAM AND HOME-MADE STRAWBERRY SAUCE

We love grilled fruit, but until recently we hadn't really figured out a good way to grill mangoes, one of our favourites. This method works well, and it creates a very unusual dessert that most of our friends really like. It can be a bit of a mess to eat, though — if that bothers you, just slice the chunks of mango into a bowl when they are cool enough after grilling, then add the ice cream and strawberry sauce.

Serves 4

THE INGREDIENTS

340g (12oz) fresh strawberries, washed, hulled, and quartered

1 tbsp granulated sugar

1 tsp fresh lime juice

2 ripe but firm mangoes

30g (1oz) unsalted butter, melted

1 litre (1¾ pints) really good vanilla ice cream, or other flavour of your choice

Build a fire in your grill. When the coals are all ignited, the flames have died down, and the temperature is medium (*see p34*), you're ready to cook.

Combine the strawberries, sugar, and lime juice in a bowl and mix well, mashing the berries up just a bit as you mix.

Cut the two halves away from the stone of each mango. For each half, crosshatch the flesh without piercing the skin, then, with your thumbs at the centre of the skin side, press each half inside-out so that it looks sort of like a hedgehog. Brush the cut sides of the mango halves lightly with butter, then put them on the grill directly over the coals, cut-side down, and cook until golden-brown (6–8 minutes). Flip them over, brush the flesh lightly with butter again, and cook until the butter just starts to caramelise (2–3 minutes more).

Place the hot, grilled mangoes cut-side up on dessert plates, top each with a scoop of ice cream, and spoon the strawberry sauce over the top.

ASH-ROASTED PEARS

As long as you've got the fire going, why not use the coals to cook dessert? This one – pears stuffed with butter and almonds and topped with flavoured whipped cream – is ideal for autumn, when pears are at their peak.

Serves 6

THE INGREDIENTS

60g (2oz) flaked almonds
6 large, firm pears
85g (3oz) unsalted butter, cut into 6 pieces
1 tbsp vanilla essence
240ml (8fl oz) well-chilled double cream
4 tbsp icing sugar
½ tsp ground cinnamon

Toast the almonds in a shallow baking tray in a 180°C (350°F/Gas 4) oven for 5–10 minutes, or very carefully in a dry frying pan on the grill, shaking frequently to avoid burning, until golden (3–5 minutes). Chop them finely in a food processor or coffee grinder.

Core the pears through the top, stopping 3mm (¼in) from the bottom. Push 1 piece of butter into the centre of each pear, along with about ⅙ of the almonds and ½ tsp vanilla.

For each pear, stack up 4 sheets of heavy-duty foil, each about 60cm (24in) long. Place the pears in the centre of the top sheets of foil, then fold up the sheets around each pear one after the other, turning the parcel a quarter-turn each time and making sure that each sheet is well-sealed around the pear.

Place the foil-wrapped pears in the coals at the periphery of the fire, where the heat is less intense. Draw the coals up around the parcels and cook until the pears are tender (15–20 minutes).

While the pears are roasting, combine the cream, icing sugar, and cinnamon in a deep bowl. Whisk with an electric mixer on medium-high speed until soft peaks form.

When the pears are tender, remove them from the coals and peel back the foil. Top each pear with a big spoonful of whipped cream and serve warm.

ASH-ROASTED APPLES

This dessert — cooked in the coals while dinner is grilling — is an extreme version of baked apples, complete with a tangy-sweet stuffing and a luscious caramel sauce. If you like, you can skip the sauce; on the other hand, you can make it hours ahead of time and just stick it in the microwave (or warm it up in a saucepan over a very low heat) right before serving dessert.

Serves 4

THE APPLES

30g (1oz) pecan nuts
4 large Golden Delicious apples (or other firm apples such as Braeburn, Orange Pippin, or Worcester Pearmain)
225g (8oz) blue cheese, crumbled
4 tbsp diced pitted dates

THE SAUCE

115g (4oz) granulated sugar
Juice of ½ orange (about 4 tbsp)
7.5cm (3in) cinnamon stick
4 tbsp double cream
Grated zest of ½ orange
Pinch of salt

Toast the pecans in a shallow baking tin in a 180°C (350°F/Gas 4) oven for 5–10 minutes, or very carefully in a dry frying pan on the grill, shaking frequently to avoid burning, until golden (3–5 minutes). Chop them finely in a food processor or coffee grinder.

Core the apples through the top, stopping 1cm (½in) from the bottom. Combine the cheese, dates, and pecans in a bowl and mix gently until evenly combined. Push a quarter of the mixture into the centre of each apple.

For each apple, stack up 4 sheets of heavy-duty foil, each about 60cm (24in) long. Place the apples in the centre of the top sheets of foil, then fold up the sheets around each apple one after the other, turning the parcel a quarter-turn each time and making sure that each sheet is well-sealed around the apple.

Place the foil-wrapped apples in the coals at the periphery of the fire, where the heat is less intense. Pile the coals up around the parcels and cook until the apples are tender (20–30 minutes).

While the apples are roasting, combine the sugar and orange juice in a small saucepan over a medium heat, stirring just until the sugar dissolves and the mixture comes to the boil. Add the cinnamon stick and simmer without stirring until the syrup turns deep amber — about 5 minutes. Remove from the heat and immediately add the cream, orange zest, and salt — the mixture will steam and sputter, and the caramel will congeal. Continue to cook, stirring gently, until the caramel dissolves completely. Set aside.

When the apples are tender, remove the parcels from the coals and cut open the foil. Remove the cinnamon stick from the caramel and drizzle the warm sauce over the apples.

GRILLED BANANA UPSIDE-DOWN CAKE

Grilled bananas bring a sweet, slightly smoky, caramelised flavour to the "topping" of this twist on a classic, created by our friend and collaborator Kirsten Mikals. Ground pecans add a little body to the cake's texture and a rich, nutty taste. If you're feeling particularly decadent, try serving this warm with a scoop of *dulce de leche* ice cream.

Serves 6–8

THE CAKE

30g (1oz) pecan nuts
115g (4oz) plain flour
2 tsp baking powder
¼ tsp salt
Pinch of ground cinnamon
85g (3oz) unsalted butter, at room temperature
180g (6oz) granulated sugar
1 large egg
1 large egg white
½ tsp vanilla essence
90ml (3fl oz) full-fat milk

THE TOPPING

3 ripe but firm bananas, unpeeled, halved lengthways
115g (4oz) soft light brown sugar
4 tbsp maple syrup
45g (1½oz) unsalted butter, plus 15g (½oz) for buttering the cake tin
¼ tsp ground allspice
Pinch of salt

Preheat the oven to 180°C (350°F/Gas 4). Butter a 23cm (9in) cake tin. Build a fire in your grill. When the coals are all ignited, the flames have died down, and the temperature is medium-hot (*see p34*), you're ready to cook.

For the topping: place the bananas on the grill over the coals, cut-side down, and cook until golden-brown and slightly charred (2–3 minutes). Set aside.

Combine the rest of the topping ingredients in a small saucepan and, on the hob, bring the mixture to a full boil over a medium-high heat, stirring until melted and smooth. Cook for 1 minute, then pour into the buttered cake tin. Peel the bananas and arrange them, grilled side down, on the syrup. Set aside.

Toast the pecans in a shallow baking tin in the oven for 5–10 minutes. Grind in a food processor or coffee grinder. Combine the ground pecans, flour, baking powder, salt, and cinnamon in a bowl and mix well.

Combine the butter and sugar in a large mixing bowl and whisk until creamy. Add the egg, egg white, and vanilla essence; whisk until light and fluffy (about 1 minute), scraping down the bowl as necessary. Add half the dry ingredients; whisk on medium speed until well-blended. Add the milk and mix well, scraping down the sides of bowl. Add the remaining dry ingredients and whisk until well-blended. Spoon the cake mix over the bananas, smoothing the surface. Bake until a toothpick inserted into the centre of the cake comes out clean (about 30 minutes).

Run a knife around the sides of the tin to loosen. Set the tin on a wire rack and let the cake cool for 15 minutes. Invert the cake onto a serving plate and carefully lift off the pan. Serve warm or at room temperature.

GRILLED PINEAPPLE AND BANANAS FOSTER

We've always liked Bananas Foster, the modern classic dessert created at Brennan's Restaurant in New Orleans. So we decided to take it in a more tropical direction by adding coconut and pineapple. And, of course, we grill the fruit. We think that the subtle smoky dimension that this brings to the dish really takes it to another level.

Serves 4

THE INGREDIENTS

2 bananas, unpeeled, halved lengthways, then halved crossways

2 slices fresh pineapple, each 1cm (½in) thick, peeled, halved, and cored

2 tbsp vegetable oil

115g (4oz) soft dark brown sugar

60g (2oz) butter

¼ tsp cinnamon

60ml (2fl oz) banana liqueur

120ml (4fl oz) your favourite dark rum

1 lime, cut in half

600ml (1 pint) your favourite ice cream

30g (1oz) toasted flaked coconut (optional)

Build a fire in your grill. When the coals are all ignited, the flames have died down, and the temperature is medium (*see p34*), you're ready to cook.

Rub the banana and pineapple slices lightly with oil and arrange them, bananas cut-side down, on the grill over the coals. Cook until the bananas are golden and the pineapple slices have light grill marks – about 2 minutes per side. Peel the bananas when they are cool enough to handle.

Combine the brown sugar, butter, and cinnamon in a large frying pan, and place it on the hob over a medium heat. When the butter and sugar are melted and very hot, mix well and add the grilled pineapple slices and peeled bananas to the frying pan, turning in the syrup to coat. Add the liqueur and rum, and as soon as the mixture starts to boil, wave a long, lit match above the surface of the syrup to ignite. Baste the fruit with the syrup until the flames die out, and immediately squeeze the lime halves over the frying pan.

Spoon the hot fruit and syrup over bowls of ice cream, sprinkle with coconut, and serve.

GRILLED GLAZED PEACHES
WITH GOAT'S CHEESE

Add a bit of sugar and black pepper to the inexpensive balsamic vinegar found in supermarkets, boil it down it until it's syrupy, and you've got yourself an easy but complex-tasting sauce. Combine this with grilled peaches and some tangy goat's cheese, and the result is a quick dessert that will knock your guests' socks off with its depth of flavour.

Serves 4

THE INGREDIENTS

240ml (8fl oz) balsamic vinegar
2 tbsp granulated sugar
1 tbsp freshly cracked black pepper
2 ripe but firm large peaches, halved and stoned
2 tbsp vegetable oil
115g (4oz) goat's cheese, crumbled

Combine the vinegar, sugar, and pepper in a small saucepan and, on the hob, bring the mixture to the boil, stirring occasionally. Reduce the heat and simmer vigorously until the mixture is syrupy and reduced by about two-thirds in volume (25–30 minutes). Remove from the heat and set aside.

Build a fire in your grill. When the coals are all ignited, the flames have died down, and the temperature is medium (see p34), you're ready to cook.

Rub the peach halves lightly with oil, then put them on the grill directly over the coals, cut-side down, and cook just until lightly seared – about 6 minutes. Flip them over, brush them generously with the glaze, and cook for 2–3 minutes more.

Place the peaches cut-side up on dessert plates and immediately top each one with a spoonful of goat's cheese. Drizzle with some additional glaze if desired, and serve warm.

POMEGRANATE LEMONADE

When you're having a barbecue and you're looking for a refreshing non-alcoholic drink that will appeal to adults, try this. The pomegranate juice adds a depth and complexity of flavour without dulling the uniquely compelling sour-sweet taste of classic still lemonade.

Makes about 2 litres (3½ pints)

225g (8oz) granulated sugar
120ml (4fl oz) water
Juice of 8 lemons (about 500ml/16fl oz)

240ml (8fl oz) pomegranate juice
1 litre (1¾ pints) cold water
Mint sprigs to garnish (optional)

In a small saucepan, combine the sugar and 120ml (4fl oz) water. Bring to the boil, stirring frequently, then lower the heat and simmer until the sugar is fully dissolved (about 1 minute). Remove from the heat and let cool to room temperature.

Fill a large pitcher halfway with ice. Add the lemon juice, pomegranate juice, cold water, and cooled syrup, and mix well.

To serve, fill tall glasses halfway with ice, and pour the lemonade over. Garnish with mint sprigs if desired.

MANGO LIMEADE

Mango juice and fresh mango give a kick of tropical flavour to traditional limeade. Although the mango is sweet, it has a kind of slightly funky flavour that keeps the drink from being too saccharine. This is a good drink for when there are a bunch of kids around — they will love it, plus they can help you squeeze all those limes.

Makes about 2 litres (3½ pints)

225g (8oz) granulated sugar
120ml (4fl oz) water
Juice of 16 limes (about 500ml/16fl oz)
240ml (8fl oz) mango juice

1 litre (1¾ pints) cold water
350g (12oz) mango, stoned and diced
Coriander sprigs to garnish (optional)

In a small saucepan, combine the sugar and water. Bring to the boil, stirring frequently, then lower the heat and simmer until the sugar is fully dissolved (about 1 minute). Remove from the heat and let cool to room temperature.

Fill a large pitcher halfway with ice. Add the lime juice, mango juice, cold water, and cooled syrup and mix well.

To serve, fill tall glasses halfway with ice, and top each with some of the diced mango. Pour the limeade over, and garnish with coriander sprigs if desired.

WATERMELON MOJITO

In our opinion, watermelon makes any summer drink more refreshing, and the mojito is no exception. This is a welcome drink before any grilled dinner, but we think it's especially delicious before any meal with Latin flavours.

Makes 1 drink

20 fresh mint leaves, a few reserved for garnishing
2 tbsp chopped fresh watermelon (without seeds),
   plus a small wedge to garnish
Juice of 1 lime (about 2 tbsp)
1 tbsp granulated sugar
60ml (2fl oz) light rum
90ml (3fl oz) soda water

Put the mint leaves, watermelon, lime juice, and sugar in a tall glass and mash them together until the mint leaves are well-bruised and the watermelon is crushed (1–2 minutes). Fill the glass with ice cubes, pour in the rum, and mix well. Top with the soda water, and garnish with a watermelon wedge and reserved mint leaves.

LYCHEE COCKTAIL

The delicate, floral sweetness of the lychee is one of Asia's most alluring flavours, so we figured it would be an excellent base for an unusual and very refreshing cocktail. You know what? We were right. This drink is particularly nice for summer parties.

Makes 1 drink

5 canned lychees, plus 1 tbsp juice from
   the can
60ml (2fl oz) vodka
30ml (1fl oz) Grand Marnier
Juice of ½ lime (about 1 tbsp)
4 mint leaves

Combine four of the lychees with the lychee juice, vodka, Grand Marnier, lime juice, mint leaves, and ice cubes in a cocktail shaker, and shake until the mixture is thoroughly combined and well-chilled (20–30 seconds). Strain into a martini glass, garnish with the remaining lychee, and serve.

EAST COAST GRILL SANGRIA

One of the most popular summer drinks at the East Coast Grill, this is a pretty straightforward version of the super-refreshing Spanish drink combining red wine and fruit, with some triple sec liqueur and brandy to deepen the flavour and add a little bit more of a kick. Bring a pitcher of this out to sip while you're grilling, and you and your guests are all going to be very happy.

Makes about 8 glasses

Plenty of ice cubes

1 bottle (750ml) dry red wine such as Beaujolais, Chianti, or Pinot Noir

Juice of 2 oranges (about 240ml/8fl oz)

120ml (4fl oz) triple sec liqueur

120ml (4fl oz) brandy

60g (2oz) granulated sugar

1 orange (unpeeled), sliced into thin rounds, rounds cut in half

240ml (8fl oz) soda water

Fill a large pitcher halfway with ice, then pour in the wine, orange juice, triple sec, brandy, and sugar. Add the orange slices and stir until the sugar dissolves and the mixture is very cold.

Pour the sangria into glasses, top each drink with a splash of soda water, and serve.

PINK SANGRIA WITH PEACHES

We've come to like rosé wines a lot lately, primarily because it's become so much easier to find good-quality ones. This combination of rosé and peaches, with citrus zing and a bit of triple sec liqueur, has got to be one of the lightest, most refreshing, but still fully satisfying drinks you'll have all summer. (Some of our friends even like it in autumn and spring.)

Makes about 8 glasses

3 ripe but firm peaches, halved and stoned

Plenty of ice cubes

1 bottle (750ml) dry rosé wine

Juice of 2 oranges (about 240ml/8fl oz)

Juice of 1 lime (about 2 tbsp)

120ml (4fl oz) triple sec liqueur

240ml (8fl oz) soda water

Dice two of the peaches small and cut the third one into eight thin wedges. Fill a large pitcher halfway with ice, then pour in the wine, orange juice, lime juice, and triple sec. Add half the diced peaches and stir until the sugar dissolves and the mixture is very cold.

Pour the sangria into glasses and add the remaining diced fruit. Top each drink with a generous splash of soda water, garnish with a peach wedge, and serve.

BLUE MARGARITA

This visually arresting cocktail may well have been responsible for starting the margarita craze when it first took hold back in the early '80s. No one is quite sure who invented it, but one thing about it is certain: it may look a little odd, but it tastes great.

Makes 1 drink

4 tbsp kosher salt (optional)
60ml (2fl oz) good-quality tequila
Juice of 2 limes (about 4 tbsp), squeezed halves
  reserved

30ml (1fl oz) blue Curaçao
1 tsp granulated sugar
1 lime slice to garnish

If you want your margarita glass salted, do it now: spread the salt in a saucer or shallow dish. Rub the rim of the glass with a reserved lime half (from making the juice), then dip the rim into the salt.

Fill the glass about halfway with ice.

Combine the tequila, lime juice, blue Curaçao, sugar, and ice cubes in a cocktail shaker, and shake until the mixture is thoroughly combined and well-chilled (20–30 seconds). Strain into the ice-filled glass and garnish with a slice of lime. Serve immediately.

CLASSIC DARK AND STORMY

The history of this ultra-simple but very delicious drink is — well, I suppose you could say it's dark and stormy. No one's quite sure where it originated, but today it's claimed as the national drink of Bermuda, and is popular in tropical locations around the world. The rich, molasses and liquorice flavour of Gosling's makes it our favourite rum for this drink, but you can use any dark rum you happen to have around.

Makes 1 drink

60ml (2fl oz) Gosling's or other dark rum
120ml (4fl oz) ginger beer
Lime wedge to garnish

Fill a tall glass about halfway with ice cubes and pour in the dark rum. Add the ginger beer, mix well, garnish with the wedge of lime, and serve.

HOT LIPS MARGARITA

We make every kind of margarita at the East Coast Grill, but this one has become a big favourite. Adding a few slices of jalapeño pepper to the mix before you shake it up imparts just the right trace of heat without rendering it undrinkably fiery.

Makes 1 drink

4 tbsp kosher salt (optional)

60ml (2fl oz) good-quality tequila

Juice of 2 limes (about 4 tbsp), squeezed halves reserved

30ml (1fl oz) triple sec liqueur

5 thin slices of red or green jalapeño pepper, or other fresh chilli pepper of your choice

1 tsp granulated sugar

1 lime slice to garnish

If you want your margarita glass salted, do it now: spread the salt in a saucer or shallow dish. Rub the rim of the glass with a reserved lime half (from making the juice), then dip the rim into the salt.

Fill the glass about halfway with ice.

Combine the tequila, lime juice, triple sec, jalapeño slices, sugar, and ice cubes in a cocktail shaker, and shake until the mixture is thoroughly combined and well-chilled (20–30 seconds). Strain into the ice-filled glass and garnish with a slice of lime. Serve immediately.

GREEN GRAPE CAIPIRINHA

Not many years ago, cachaça, the distilled sugar cane spirit from Brazil, was popular only in that country, where per capita consumption runs to about three gallons per year. But the recent popularity of the caipirinha cocktail has given this spirit a worldwide reputation. Here we substitute green grapes for the lime used in the traditional version, which gives a slightly sweeter, more subtle flavour.

Makes 1 drink

8 green grapes, halved

1½ tbsp granulated sugar

60ml (2fl oz) cachaça

Combine the grapes and sugar in an old-fashioned glass and mash them together until the grapes are pretty well smashed (at least 1 minute). Fill the glass with ice cubes, pour in the cachaça, mix well, and serve.

INDEX

ACKNOWLEDGMENTS.

AUTHORS' ACKNOWLEDGMENTS

FROM BOTH OF US

Thanks to our inimitable agent, the indefatigable Doe Coover, who keeps finding new avenues for us to ply our trade. Also, thanks to Kirsten Mikalson and Nancy Boyce who were indispensable aides in transfering the recipes in this book from mind to paper. And to all the folks at DK and Cobalt, in particular Louise Abbott, for putting together a beautiful book that actually makes sense. And, of course, thanks to Rick and Susan, Tommy, Lizzie, and Josh, and Owen T.

FROM CHRIS

To own a restaurant and be able to do anything but run the restaurant 24/7 is a luxury that is not afforded to most folks in the business. To my good fortune, at the East Coast Grill I work with a group of people whose diligence, dedication, and hard work allow me to pursue projects outside of the restaurant. To them I say: you are awesome, thanks for making me look good, and don't go changin'. Special shout-outs to Chefs Eric Gburski and Jason Lord, General Manager Kristi Morris, and CFO Laurie Govoni.

Collaborating on a book is an arduous task in any event, but over my cookbook-writing career I have been privileged to work with the accomplished wordsmith, Doc Willoughby, whose sharp eye, quick wit, and cool Manhattan apartment make for a pleasurable partnership. Doc, you always do more than your share of the work without too much complaning. Thanks for that and thanks for the laughs.

FROM DOC

Thanks to Ruth, Larry, and all the other folks at *Gourmet* for their patience and forbearance as I worked my way through this book. And to Mark Bittman for helping me keep perspective on the whole thing. Thanks, too, to my faithful dining companions Tucker, Chris I, Francis, Richard, and Bobby, and to Dave for keeping me from getting too fat.

Creating books with my friend Chris has always been as much fun as it is work. His lifelong slogan, "Work smarter, not harder," translates into more exciting dinners and cool excursions than a cookbook author has any right to expect. Not to mention that his recipes rock. Thanks, Chris, for your good humor, sense of adventure, and steadfast friendship.

PUBLISHER'S ACKNOWLEDGMENTS

Cobalt id would like to thank the following for their help with this book: Sarah Tomley for editorial assistance; Christy Lusiak and Charles Wills for proofreading and US liaison; and Hilary Bird for indexing. Our thanks also to Briar Towers at Dorling Kindersley, and especially to Ian O'Leary, photography assistant Gemma Reynolds, and stylist Gizzi Erskine, who is represented by HERS (hersagency.co.uk).